101 Traditional Christmas Carols

Copyright © 2022 Our World

All rights reserved.

101 Traditional Christmas Carols

This book is dedicated to Jesus Christ, our savior.

Contents

1.	A Great and Mighty Wonder	1
2.	An Angel This Night	2
3.	The Kerry Christmas Carol	4
4.	Angels from the Realms of Glory	5
5.	Angels We Have Heard on High	7
6.	As with Gladness Men of Old	8
7.	Away In A Manger	9
8.	Beautiful Star Of Bethlehem	10
9.	Behold Three Kings Come From the East	11
10.	Bethlehem Down	12
11.	The Boars Head Carol	13
12.	Brightest and Best	14
13.	Calypso Carol	15
14.	Candlelight Carol	16
15.	Carol of the Bells	17
16.	Children Go Where I Send Thee	19
17.	Christians, awake! salute the happy morn	22
18.	Christmas Day Is Come	23
19.	Come and I will sing you	26
20.	Come, Thou Long Expected Jesus	27
21.	Coventry Carol	28
22.	Curoo Curoo	29
23.	Ding Dong Merrily on High	31
24.	Do You Hear What I Hear	31
25.	Down in Yon Forest	33

26.	Far, Far Away on Judea's Plains	34
27.	Gabriel's Message	36
28.	Gloucestershire Wassail	37
29.	Go Tell It on the Mountain	39
30.	God Rest Ye Merry, Gentlemen	40
31.	Go Tell It on the Mountain	42
32.	Good King Wenceslas	43
33.	Hail Ye Flowers of Martyrs	45
34.	Hark! The Herald Angels Sing	46
35.	Here We Come A-wassailing	47
36.	I Heard the Bells on Christmas Day	49
37.	I Saw Three Ships (Come Sailing In)	51
38.	I Wonder as I Wander	52
39.	In the Bleak Midwinter	53
40.	Infant Holy, Infant Lowly	55
41.	It Came Upon the Midnight Clear	56
42.	Jerusalem, Our Happy Home	57
43.	Jesus Christ the Apple Tree	59
44.	Jingle Bells	60
45.	Joy to the World	62
46.	Judea	64
47.	Little Donkey	65
48.	Love Came Down at Christmas	66
49.	Mary's Boy Child	67
50.	Masters in this hall	68
51.	Silent night	70
52.	Now To Conclude Our Christmas Mirth	71
53.	In Dulci Jubilo	74

54.	O come, O come, Emmanuel	75
55.	O Holy Night	76
56.	O Little Town of Bethlehem	77
57.	Of the Father's Heart Begotten (Of the Father's Love Begotten)	79
58.	Once in Royal David's City	82
59.	Past Three O'Clock (or Past Three a Clock)	83
60.	Rise Up Shepherd and Foller	85
61.	Rudolph, the Red-Nosed Reindeer	86
62.	Sans Day Carol	88
63.	See, amid the Winter's Snow	89
64.	Shepherds Arise	91
65.	Silver Bells	92
66.	Sir Christèmas	92
67.	St John did Lean on Jesus' Breast	93
68.	Star of the East	94
69.	Sweet Jesus Was the Sacred Name	96
70.	Sweet Little Jesus Boy	97
71.	Sweetest of All Names, Jesus	98
72.	The Angel Said to Joseph Mild	100
73.	The Babe in Bethlem's Manger	101
74.	The Cherry-Tree Carol	102
75.	The Darkest Midnight in December	103
76.	The First Noel (The First Nowell)	107
77.	The Friendly Beasts	108
78.	The Holly and the Ivy	110
79.	The Little Drummer Boy	112
80.	The Lord at first did Adam make	114
81.	The Rocking Carol	116

#	Title	Page
82.	The Seven Joys of Mary	116
83.	There Is No Rose	118
84.	This Endris Night	119
85.	This is St Stephen's Day	122
86.	To Greet Our Saviour's Dear	123
87.	Torches	126
88.	Unto Us a Boy is Born (Unto Us is Born a Son)	127
89.	We Three Kings of Orient Are	128
90.	Wexford Carol	130
91.	What Child Is This?	131
92.	Whence Is That Lovely Fragrance	132
93.	While by My Sheep I Watched at Night	133
94.	While Shepherds Watched Their Flocks	134
95.	With Wondering Awe, the Wisemen Saw	135
96.	Ye Sons of Men with Me Rejoice	136
97.	In the Bleak Mid-Winter	141
98.	O Come All Ye Faithful	143
99.	What Sweeter Music	144
100.	Sussex Carol	146
101.	Virgin Unspotted (A Virgin Most Pure)	147

1. A Great and Mighty Wonder

A great and mighty wonder
Our Christmas festal brings:
On earth a lowly infant
Behold the King of kings!

The Word is made incarnate
Descending from on high;
And cherubim sing anthems
To shepherds from the sky

And we with them, triumphant
Repeat the hymn again:
"To God on high be glory
And peace on earth to men! "

While thus they sing your Monarch
Those bright angelic bands
Rejoice, ye vales and mountains!
Ye oceans, clap your hands!

Since all He comes to ransom
By all be He adored;
The Infant born in Bethlehem
The Savior and the Lord!

And idol forms shall perish
And error shall decay
And Christ shall wield His scepter
Our Lord and God for aye...

2. An Angel This Night

An angel this night doth to the shepherds bring
Most rare and joyful news to move all hearts to sing:
A Saviour from heaven unto the world is come,
And God is now made Man for man's redemption.

The shepherds in haste unto the stable run
To see this precious Child, the eternal Father's Son;
Without a father born, His Mother a pure maid,
By whom this heavenly Babe is in a manger laid.

Now let us with the shepherds unto the stable go,
Those miracles and wonders for to adore and know,
With humble wit and will and open eyes of faith,
We shall believe and see all that the angel saith.

But wits of men and angels cannot conceive this bliss,
No heart can full resent it, no tongue tell what it is,
Wits must admire and marvel and hearts astonished be,
And tongues with joy be silent in this great mystery.

Here all the hopes of earth and the delights of heaven,
The joy of all the angels and the great price of man,
The ransom of all sinners, all captives to set free,
How can we but rejoice and all must merry be.

How can we but rejoice to hear what now is done,
The Son of God made man andrnan made God's true Son:
God doth appear on earth for to raise earth to heaven,
What cause of greater joy could ever happen men?

Now infinite height is low and infinite depth is shallow,
The greatest length is short, the greatest largeness narrow,
Eternity by time is measured and closed up,
Immensity confined and in a stable shut.

The increated Person is now created Man,
The Creator made Creature, who shall these secrets scan?
Who made all things of nothing, a nothing is become,
Our God most high and great is a poor Virgin's son.

His greatness is made humble and all His might is weak,
His glory is obscured, His wisdom doth not speak,
His pleasures do suffer, His treasures are in want.
He made and rules the world and yet He's bare and scant:

But 'tis to strengthen us His might is made so weak,
'Tis for our faults and folly His wisdom doth not speak;
For to correct our pride in humble sort He lies,
And for to make us rich, most poor He lives and dies.

The angels may admire how these strange things can be,
And all the devils may tremble, their terrors for to see;
But sinners all on earth may well rejoice and sing,
To thank and praise and glorify their Saviour and their King.

Then glory unto the Father Who ordered all things thus,
Glory unto the Son Who gave Himself for us,
Glory to the Holy Ghost Who did this work of heaven,
Glory unto Them now and evermore. Amen.

3. The Kerry Christmas Carol

Brush the floor and clean the hearth and set the fire to keep
For they might visit us tonight when all the world's asleep.
Don't blow the tall white candle out but leave it burning bright
So that they'll know they're welcome here this holy Christmas night.

Leave out the bread and meat for them and sweet milk for the Child
And they will bless the fire that baked and too the hands that toiled
For Joseph will be travel-tired and Mary pale and wan

And they can sleep a little while before they journey on.
They will be weary of the roads and rest will comfort them
For it must be many a lonely mile from here to Bethlehem.
O long the road they have to go the bad mile with the good
Till the journey ends on Calvary beneath a Cross of wood.

So leave the door upon the latch and set the fire to keep
And pray they'll rest with us tonight when all the world's asleep.
Don't blow the tall white candle out but leave it burning bright
So that they'll know they're welcome here this holy Christmas night.

4. Angels from the Realms of Glory

Angels from the realms of glory,
Wing your flight o'er all the earth;
Ye who sang creation's story,
Now proclaim Messiah's birth:
Come and worship,
Come and worship,
Worship Christ, the newborn King!

Shepherds, in the fields abiding,
Watching o'er your flocks by night,
God with man is now residing,
Yonder shines the infant Light;
Come and worship,
Come and worship,
Worship Christ, the newborn King!

Sages, leave your contemplations,
Brighter visions beam afar;
Seek the great desire of nations,
Ye have seen His natal star;
Come and worship,
Come and worship,
Worship Christ, the newborn King!

Saints before the altar bending,
Watching long in hope and fear,
Suddenly the Lord, descending,
In His temple shall appear:
Come and worship,
Come and worship,
Worship Christ, the newborn King!

5. Angels We Have Heard on High

Angels we have heard on high
Sweetly singing o'er the plains
And the mountains in reply
Echoing their joyous strains

[Chorus]
Gloria In Excelsis Deo
Gloria In Excelsis Deo

Shepherds why this jubilee?
Why your joyous strains prolong?
Say what may the tidings be
Which inspire your heavenly song?

Gloria In Excelsis Deo
Gloria In Excelsis Deo

Come to Bethlehem and see
Him Whose birth the angels sing;
Come, adore on bended knee
Christ the Lord, the newborn King

6. As with Gladness Men of Old

As with gladness, men of old
Did the guiding star behold;
As with joy they hailed its light,
Leading onward, beaming bright;
So, most gracious Lord, may we
Evermore be led to Thee.

As with joyful steps they sped
To that lowly manger-bed;
There to bend the knee before
Him Whom heaven and earth adore;
So may we with willing feet
Ever seek the mercy-seat.

As they offered gifts most rare
At that manger rude and bare;
So may we, with holy joy,
Pure and free from sin's alloy,
All our costliest treasures bring,
Christ! to Thee our heavenly King.

Holy Jesus, every day
Keep us in the narrow way;
And, when earthly things are past,
Bring our ransomed souls at last

Where they need no star to guide,
Where no clouds Thy Glory hide.

In the heavenly country bright,
Need they no created light;
Thou its Light, its Joy, its Crown,
Thou its Sun which goes not down;
There for ever may we sing
Alleluias to our King.

7. Away In A Manger

Away in a manger, no crib for a bed,
The little Lord Jesus laid down his sweet head.
The stars in the sky looked down where he lay,
The little Lord Jesus asleep in the hay.

The cattle are lowing, the baby awakes,
But little Lord Jesus no crying he makes.
I love Thee, Lord Jesus, look down from the sky
And stay by my cradle til morning is nigh.

Be near me, Lord Jesus, I ask Thee to stay
Close by me forever, and love me, I pray.
Bless all the dear children in thy tender care,
And take us to heaven, to live with Thee there.

8. Beautiful Star Of Bethlehem

Oh Beautiful Star of Bethlehem
Shining afar through shadows dim
Giving the light for those who long have gone
Guiding the wise men on their way
Unto the place where Jesus lay
Oh Beautiful Star of Bethlehem shine on.

Oh Beautiful Star of Bethlehem   (Star of Bethlehem)
Shine upon us until the glory dawns.
Give us a light to guide the way
Unto the land of perfect day
Oh Beautiful Star of Bethlehem, shine on (shine on)

Oh Beautiful Star the hope of light
Guiding the pilgrims through the night
Over the mountains till the break of dawn
Into the light of perfect day
It will give out a lovely ray
Oh Beautiful Star of Bethlehem shine on (shine on)

Oh Beautiful Star the hope of rest
For the redeemed the good and blessed
Yonder in glory when the crown is won
Jesus is now the star divine
Brighter and brighter he will shine
Oh Beautiful Star of Bethlehem shine on (shine on)

9. Behold Three Kings Come From the East

Behold three kings came from the east,
Led by a star of stars the best,
Which brought them where they did espy
The King of Kings and Saviour lie;
With gold and myrh and frankincense,
They did adore this new-born Prince.

It's strange what did these three kings see
That might by them adored be,
A tender Babe laid on the ground,
Yet they submit, sceptre and crown
Their gold, their myrh, their frankincense,
For to adore this new-born Prince.

Then let us with those three kings bring
Our gifts unto this new-born King,
Our sense, our will, our wit, our heart,
And all that e'er we can impart;
Our gold, our myrh, our frankincense,
For to adore this new-born Prince.

10. Bethlehem Down

When He is King we will give Him a King's gifts,
Myrrh for its sweetness, and gold for a crown,
Beautiful robes", said the young girl to Joseph,
Fair with her first-born on Bethlehem Down.

Bethlehem Down is full of the starlight,
Winds for the spices, and stars for the gold,
Mary for sleep, and for lullaby music,
Songs of a shepherd by Bethlehem fold.

When He is King they will clothe Him in grave-sheets,
Myrrh for embalming, and wood for a crown,
He that lies now in the white arms of Mary,
Sleeping so lightly on Bethlehem Down

Here He has peace and a short while for dreaming,
Close-huddled oxen to keep him from cold,
Mary for love, and for lullaby music,
Songs of a shepherd by Bethlehem Down.

11. The Boars Head Carol

The boar's head in hand bring I,
Bedeck'd with bays and rosemary.
I pray you, my masters, be merry
Quot estis in convivio

Caput apri defero
Reddens laudes Domino

The boar's head, as I understand,
Is the rarest dish in all this land,
Which thus bedeck'd with a gay garland
Let us servire cantico.

Caput apri defero
Reddens laudes Domino

Our steward hath provided this
In honor of the King of Bliss;
Which, on this day to be served is
In Reginensi atrio.

Caput apri defero
Reddens laudes Domino

12.   Brightest and Best

Brightest and Best of the sons of the morning,
Dawn on our darkness and lend us Thine aid;
Star of the East, the horizon adorning,
Guide where our infant Redeemer is laid.

Cold on His cradle the dewdrops are shining;
Low lies His head with the beasts of the stall;
Angels adore Him in slumber reclining,
Maker and Monarch and Savior of all!

Say, shall we yield Him, in costly devotion,
Odors of Edom and offerings divine?
Gems of the mountain and pearls of the ocean,
Myrrh from the forest, or gold from the mine?

Vainly we offer each ample oblation,
Vainly with gifts would His favor secure;
Richer by far is the heart's adoration,
Dearer to God are the prayers of the poor.

13. Calypso Carol

See him alying on a bed of straw;
Draughty stable with an open door,
Mary cradling the babe she bore;
The prince of glory is his name.

Refrain
Oh, now carry me to Bethlehem
to see the Lord appear to men;
Just as poor as was the stable then,
The prince of glory when he came.

Star of silver sweep across the skies,
show where Jesus in the manger lies.
Shepherds swiftly from your stupor rise
to see the Saviour of the world.

Mine are riches from thy poverty,
From thine innocence, eternity;
Mine, forgiveness by thy death for me,
Child of sorrow for my joy.

Angels, sing agan the song you sang,
bring God's glory to the heart of man;
Sing the Bethl'hem's little baby can
be salvation to the soul.

14. Candlelight Carol

How do you capture the wind on the water?
How do you count all the stars in the sky?
How can you measure the love of a mother?
Or how can you write down a baby's first cry?

Candlelight, angel light, firelight and star-glow
Shine on his cradle 'til breaking of dawn
Gloria, gloria in excelsis Deo!
Angels are singing "The Christ child is born"
(Angels are singing "The Christ child is born")

Shepherds and wise men will kneel and adore him
Seraphim 'round him, their vigil will keep
Nations proclaim him their Lord and their saviour
But Mary will hold him and sing him to sleep

Candlelight, angel light, firelight and star-glow
Shine on his cradle 'til breaking of dawn
Gloria, gloria in excelsis Deo!
Angels are singing "The Christ child is born"

Find him in Bethlehem laid in a manger
Christ our redeemer, asleep in the hay
Godhead incarnate and hope of salvation
A child with his mother that first Christmas Day

Candlelight, angel light, firelight and star-glow
Shine on his cradle 'til breaking of dawn
Gloria, gloria in excelsis Deo!
Angels are singing "The Christ child is born"
Angels are singing "The Christ child is born"

15. Carol of the Bells

Hark how the bells,
sweet silver bells,
all seem to say,
throw cares away

Christmas is here,
bringing good cheer,
to young and old,
meek and the bold.

Ding dong ding dong
that is their song
with joyful ring
all caroling.

One seems to hear
words of good cheer

from everywhere
filling the air.

Oh how they pound,
raising the sound,
o'er hill and dale,
telling their tale.

Gaily they ring
while people sing
songs of good cheer,
Christmas is here.
Merry, Merry, Merry, Merry Christmas,
Merry, Merry, Merry, Merry Christmas.

On on they send,
on without end,
their joyful tone
to every home.
Ding ding... dong!

16. Children Go Where I Send Thee

Children go where I send thee
How shall I send thee?

I'm gonna send you one by one
One for the little bitty baby
Born of the Virgin Mary
Born, born, born in Bethlehem

Children go where I send thee
How shall I send thee?

I'm gonna send you two by two
Two for Paul and Silas
One for the little bitty baby
Born of the Virgin Mary
Born, born, born in Bethlehem

Children go where I send thee
How shall I send thee?

I'm gonna send you three by three
Three for the Hebrew children
Two for Paul and Silas
One for the little bitty baby
Born of the Virgin Mary
Born, born, born in Bethlehem

Children go where I send thee
How shall I send thee?

I'm gonna send you four by four
Four for the four knocking on the door
Three for the Hebrew children
Two for Paul and Silas
One for the little bitty baby
Born of the Virgin Mary
Born, born, born in Bethlehem

Children go where I send thee
How shall I send thee?

I'm gonna send you five by five
Five for the gospel preachers
Four for the four knocking on the door
Three for the Hebrew children
Two for Paul and Silas
One for the little bitty baby
Born of the Virgin Mary
Born, born, born in Bethlehem

Children go where I send thee
How shall I send thee?

I'm gonna send you six by six

Six for the six that couldn't get fixed
Five for the gospel preachers
Four for the four knocking on the door
Three for the Hebrew children
Two for Paul and Silas
One for the little bitty baby
Born of the Virgin Mary
Born, born, born in Bethlehem

Children go where I send thee
How shall I send thee?

I'm gonna send you seven by seven
Seven for the seven that all went to Heaven
Six for the six that couldn't get fixed
Five for the gospel preachers
Four for the four knocking on the door
Three for the Hebrew children
Two for Paul and Silas
One for the little bitty baby
Born of the Virgin Mary
Born, born, born in Bethlehem

Children go where I send thee
How shall I send thee?

I'm gonna send you eight by eight
Eight for the eight that stood at the gate

Seven for the seven that all went to Heaven
Six for the six that couldn't get fixed
Five for the gospel preachers
Four for the four knocking on the door
Three for the Hebrew children
Two for Paul and Silas
One for the little bitty baby
Born of the Virgin Mary
Born, born, born in Bethlehem

He was born, born in Bethlehem!

17. Christians, awake! salute the happy morn

Christians, awake, salute the happy morn,
whereon the Savior of the world was born;
rise to adore the mystery of love,
which hosts of angels chanted from above;
with them the joyful tidings were begun
of God incarnate and the Virgin's son.

Then to the watchful shepherds it was told,
who heard th'angelic herald's voice: "Behold,

I bring good tidings of a Savior's birth
to you and all the nations on the earth:
this day hath God fulfilled his promised word,
this day is born a Savior, Christ the Lord."

He spake, and straightway the celestial choir
in hymns of joy, unknown before, conspire;
the praises of redeeming love they sang,
and heav'n's whole orb with alleluias rang;
God's highest glory was their anthem still,
peace on the earth, and unto men good will.

18. Christmas Day Is Come

Christmas Day is come; Let us prepare for mirth,
Which fills the Heav'ns and Earth, At His amazing Birth.
Through both thy joyous angels, In strife and hurry fly,
With glory and Hosannas, Holy, Holy they cry.
In Heav'n the church triumphant ,Adores with all her choirs,
The militant on earth, With humble faith admires.

But how can we rejoice, should we not rather mourn
To see the Hope of nations thus in a stable born?
Where is His crown and sceptre, where is His throne

sublime?
Where is his train and majesty that should the stars outshine?
Is there no sumptuous palace, is there no inn at all
To lodge His heavenly Mother—but in a filthy stall?

Why does He thus demean, or thus Himself disguise?
Perhaps He would conceal Himself from cruel enemies.
He trusts but two dumb beasts afeeding on their hay:
He steals to us at midnight that none should Him betray.
And His Supposed father a carpenter must be,
That none should yet discover the sacred mystery.

Yet He does not intend to shun His fate decreed;
His death must be the ransom by which mankind is freed.
With a long course of suffering for thirty years and three.
Which must be all completed upon Mount Calvary.
For these He now reserves Himself, contented to begin
In poverty and misery to pay for all our sin.

Cease ye blessed angels such clamorous joys to make;
Though midnight silence favours, the shepherds are awake;
And you, O glorious star, that with new splendour brings
From the remotest parts three learned eastern Kings,
Turn someway else your lustre, your rays elsewhere display,
Herod will slay the Babe, and Christ must straight away.

Alas! to teeming nature we offer rules in vain,

When big with such a prodigy it can't itself contain:
The rocks were split asunder to grieve our Saviour's death,
And at His Resurrection the dead sprung from the earth.
Can we now expect that on His joyful birth,
The creatures should conceal their triumph and their mirth?

Then let our joys abound, now all His griefs are o'er;
His victory we celebrates His sufferings we deplore.
This was the toil and slavery that getting was for us;
Yo're welcome, thrice welcome, Divine Saviour Jesus!
Your Christmas is in glory. your torments are all past;
Whate'er betide us now grant us the same at last.

If we would rejoice let us cancel the old score,
And purposing amendment, resolve to Sin no more.
For mirth can ne'er content without a conscience clear;
You shall not find trite pleasure in all the usual cheer,
In dancing, sporting, revelling with masquerade and drum;
Then let our Christmas merry be as Christians doth become.

19. Come and I will sing you

Come and I will sing you
What will I sing you?
I will sing you one -o
What will the one be?
One the one that's all alone and ever more will be so

Come and I will sing you
What will I sing you?
I will sing you two-o
What will the two be?
Two of them were lily white babes, clothed all in green-o
One the one that's all alone and ever more shall be so

Come and I will sing you
What will I sing you?
I will sing you three-o
What will the three be?
Three of them were drivers
Two of them were lily white babes, clothed all in green-o
One the one that's all alone and ever more shall be so

Come and I will sing you
What will I sing you?
I will sing you four-o
What will the four be?
Four gospel preachers

Three of them were drivers
Two of them were lily white babes, clothed all in green-o
One the one that's all alone and ever more shall be so

20. Come, Thou Long Expected Jesus

Come, thou long expected Jesus,
Born to set thy people free;
From our fears and sins release us;
Let us find our rest in thee.
Israel's strength and consolation,
Hope of all the earth Thou art;
Dear Desire of ev'ry nation,
Joy of every longing heart.

Joy to those who long to see Thee
Day-spring from on high, appear.
Come, Thou promised Rod of Jesse,
Of Thy birth, we long to hear!
O'er the hills the angels singing
News, glad tidings of a birth;
"Go to Him your praises bringing
Christ the Lord has come to earth!"

Come to earth to taste our sadness,
He whose glories knew no end.
By His life He brings us gladness,
Our redeemer, Shepherd, Friend.
Leaving riches without number,
Born within a cattle stall;
This the everlasting wonder,
Christ was born the Lord of all.

Born thy people to deliver,
Born a child, and yet a King,
Born to reign in us for ever,
Now Thy gracious kingdom bring.
By thine own eternal Spirit
Rule in all our hearts alone;
By thine all-sufficient merit
Raise us to thy glorious throne.

21. Coventry Carol

Lully, lullay, Thou little tiny Child,
Bye, bye, lully, lullay.
Lullay, thou little tiny Child,
Bye, bye, lully, lullay.

O sisters too, how may we do,
For to preserve this day
This poor youngling for whom we do sing
Bye, bye, lully, lullay.

Herod, the king, in his raging,
Charged he hath this day
His men of might, in his own sight,
All children young to slay.

That woe is me, poor Child for Thee!
And ever mourn and sigh,
For thy parting neither say nor sing,
Bye, bye, lully, lullay.

22. Curoo Curoo

For many a bird did wake and fly
Curoo, curoo, curoo
For many a bird did wake and fly
To a manger bed with a wandering cry
On Christmas day in the morning
Curoo, curoo, curoo
Curoo, curoo, curoo

The lark, the dove, the red bird came
Curoo, curoo, curoo
The lark, the dove, the red bird came
And they did sing in sweet Jesus' name
On Christmas day in the morning
Curoo, curoo, curoo
Curoo, curoo, curoo

The owl was there with eyes so wide
Curoo, curoo, curoo
The owl was there with eyes so wide
And he did sing at sweet Mary's side
On Christmas day in the morning
Curoo, curoo, curoo
Curoo, curoo, curoo

The shepherds knelt upon the hay
Curoo, curoo, curoo
The shepherds knelt upon the hay
And the angels sang the night away
On Christmas day in the morning
Curoo, curoo, curoo
Curoo, curoo, curoo

23. Ding Dong Merrily on High

Ding dong merrily on high
In heaven the bells are ringing
Ding dong, verily the sky
Is riven with angel singing.
Gloria, Hosanna in excelsis

Even so here below, below
Let steeple bells be swungen
And "Io, io, io"
By priest and people sungen
Gloria, Hosanna in excelsis
Pray you, dutifully prime
Your matin' chime, ye ringers
May you beautifully rime
Your evetime song, ye singers
Gloria, Hosanna in excelsis

24. Do You Hear What I Hear

Said the night wind to the little lamb:
"Do you see what I see?
Way up in the sky, little lamb
Do you see what I see?

A star, a star, dancing in the night
With a tail as big as a kite
With a tail as big as a kite"

Said the little lamb to the shepherd boy:
"Do you hear what I hear?
Ringing through the sky, shepherd boy
Do you hear what I hear?
A song, a song, high above the trees
With a voice as big as the sea
With a voice as big as the sea"

Said the shepherd boy to the mighty king:
"Do you know what I know?
In your palace warm, mighty king
Do you know what I know?
A Child, a Child shivers in the cold
Let us bring Him silver and gold
Let us bring Him silver and gold"

Said the king to the people everywhere:
"Listen to what I say!
Pray for peace, people everywhere!
Listen to what I say!
The Child, the Child, sleeping in the night
He will bring us goodness and light
He will bring us goodness and light"

25. Down in Yon Forest

Down in yon forest be a hall,
Sing May, Queen May, sing Mary!
'Tis coverlided over with purple and pall.
Sing all good men for the new-born Baby!

Oh in that hall is a pallet bed,
Sing May, Queen May, sing Mary!
'Tis stained with blood like cardinal red.
Sing all good men for the new-born Baby!

And at that pallet is a stone
Sing May, Queen May, sing Mary!
On which the Virgin did atone
Sing all good men for the new-born Baby!

Under that Hall is a gushing flood
Sing May, Queen May, sing Mary!
From Christ's own side 'tis water and blood.
Sing all good men for the new-born Baby!

Beside that bed a shrub tree grows,
Sing May, Queen May, sing Mary!
Since He was born it blooms and blows.
Sing all good men for the new-born Baby!

Oh, on that bed a young Squire sleeps,

Sing May, Queen May, sing Mary!
His wounds are sick, and see, he weeps.
Sing all good men for the new-born Baby!

Oh hail yon Hall were none can sin,
Sing May, Queen May, sing Mary!
Cause it's gold outside and silver within,
Sing all good men for the new-born Baby!

26. Far, Far Away on Judea's Plains

Far, far away on Judea's plains,
Shepherds of old
Heard the joyous strains:
Glory to God, Glory to God,
Glory to God in the highest:
Peace on earth,
Good-will to men;
Peace on earth,
Good-will to men!

Sweet are these strains
Of redeeming love,
Message of mercy from heaven above:

Glory to God, Glory to God,
Glory to God in the highest:
Peace on earth,
Good-will to men;
Peace on earth,

Lord, with the angels
We too would rejoice,
Help us to sing with
The heart and voice:
Glory to God, Glory to God,
Glory to God in the highest:
Peace on earth,
Good-will to men;
Peace on earth,
Good-will to men!

Hasten the time when,
From every clime,
Men shall unite
In the strains sublime:
Glory to God, Glory to God,
Glory to God in the highest:
Peace on earth,
Good-will to men;
Peace on earth,
Good-will to men!

27. Gabriel's Message

The angel Gabriel from heaven came,
His wings as drifted snow, his eyes as flame,
All hail, said he, thou lowly maiden Mary!
Most highly favoured Lady, Gloria!

For known a blessed mother thou shalt be,
All generations laud and honour thee,
Thy son shall be Emmanuel by seers foretold,
Most highly favoured Lady, Gloria!

Then gentle Mary meekly bowed her head,
"To me be as it pleaseth God," she said,
"my soul shall laud and magnify his holy Name."
Most highly favoured Lady, Gloria!

Of her, Emmanuel, the Christ, was born
in Bethlehem, all on a Christmas morn,
and Christian folk throughout the world will ever say,
Most highly favoured Lady, Gloria!

28. Gloucestershire Wassail

Wassail! wassail! all over the town,
Our toast it is white and our ale it is brown;
Our bowl it is made of the white maple tree;
With the wassailing bowl1, we'll drink to thee.

Here's to our horse, and to his right ear,
God send our master a happy new year:
A happy new year as e'er he did see,
With my wassailing bowl I drink to thee.

So here is to Cherry and to his right cheek
Pray God send our master a good piece of beef
And a good piece of beef that may we all see
With the wassailing bowl, we'll drink to thee.

Here's to our mare, and to her right eye,
God send our mistress a good Christmas pie;
A good Christmas pie as e'er I did see,
With my wassailing bowl I drink to thee.

So here is to Broad Mary and to her broad horn
May God send our master a good crop of corn
And a good crop of corn that may we all see
With the wassailing bowl, we'll drink to thee.

And here is to Fillpail and to her left ear

Pray God send our master a happy New Year
And a happy New Year as e'er he did see
With the wassailing bowl, we'll drink to thee.

Here's to our cow, and to her long tail,
God send our master us never may fail
Of a cup of good beer: I pray you draw near,
And our jolly wassail it's then you shall hear.

Come butler, come fill us a bowl of the best
Then we hope that your soul in heaven may rest
But if you do draw us a bowl of the small
Then down shall go butler, bowl and all.

Be here any maids? I suppose here be some;
Sure they will not let young men stand on the cold stone!
Sing hey O, maids! come trole back the pin,
And the fairest maid in the house let us all in.

Then here's to the maid in the lily white smock
Who tripped to the door and slipped back the lock
Who tripped to the door and pulled back the pin
For to let these jolly wassailers in.

29. Go Tell It on the Mountain

Go, tell it on the mountain
Over the hills and everywhere
Go, tell it on the mountain
That Jesus Christ is born

While shepherds kept their watching
O'er silent flocks by night
Behold throughout the heavens
There shone a Holy light

Go, tell it on the mountain
Over the hills and everywhere
Go, tell it on the mountain
That Jesus Christ is born

The shepherds feared and trembled
When, lo! Above the Earth
Rang out the angel chorus
That hailed our Savior's birth

Go, tell it on the mountain
Over the hills and everywhere
Go, tell it on the mountain
That Jesus Christ is born

Down in a lowly manger

Our humble Christ was born
And brought us all salvation
That blessed Christmas morn

Go, tell it on the mountain
Over the hills and everywhere
Go, tell it on the mountain
That Jesus Christ is born
That Jesus Christ is born

30. God Rest Ye Merry, Gentlemen

God rest ye merry gentlemen
Let nothing you dismay
Remember Christ our Savior
Was born on Christmas Day
To save us all from Satan's pow'r
When we were gone astray
Oh tidings of comfort and joy
Comfort and joy
Oh tidings of comfort and joy
God rest ye merry gentlemen
Let nothing you dismay
Remember Christ our Savior

Was born on Christmas Day
To save us all from Satan's pow'r
When we were gone astray
Oh tidings of comfort and joy
Comfort and joy
Oh tidings of comfort and joy

In Bethlehem, in Israel
This blessed Babe was born
And laid within a manger
Upon this blessed morn
The which His Mother Mary
Did nothing take in scorn
Oh tidings of comfort and joy
Comfort and joy
Oh tidings of comfort and joy

Fear not then, said the Angel
Let nothing you affright
This day is born a Savior
Of a pure Virgin bright
To free all those who trust in Him
From Satan's pow'r and might
Oh tidings of comfort and joy
Comfort and joy
Oh tidings of comfort and joy

God rest ye merry gentlemen

Let nothing you dismay
Remember Christ our Savior
Was born on Christmas Day
To save us all from Satan's pow'r
When we were gone astray
Oh tidings of comfort and joy
Comfort and joy
Oh tidings of comfort and joy

31. Go Tell It on the Mountain

Good Christian men, rejoice
With heart, and soul, and voice;
Give ye heed to what we say:
News! News!
Jesus Christ was born to-day:
Ox and ass before Him bow,
And He is in the manger now.
Christ is born today! Christ is born today.

Good Christian men, rejoice,
With heart, and soul, and voice;
Now ye hear of endless bliss:
Joy! Joy!

Jesus Christ was born for this!
He hath ope'd the heav'nly door,
And man is blessed evermore.
Christ was born for this! Christ was born for this!

Good Christian men, rejoice
With heart, and soul, and voice;
Now ye need not fear the grave:
Peace! Peace!
Jesus Christ was born to save!
Calls you one, and calls you all,
To gain His everlasting hall:
Christ was born to save! Christ was born to save!

32. Good King Wenceslas

Good King Wenceslas looked out
On the Feast of Stephen
When the snow lay round about
Deep and crisp and even
Brightly shone the moon that night
Though the frost was cruel
When a poor man came in sight
Gathering winter fuel

Hither, page, and stand by me,
If thou knowst it, telling
Yonder peasant, who is he?
Where and what his dwelling?
Sire, he lives a good league hence,
Underneath the mountain
Right against the forest fence
By Saint Agnes fountain.

Bring me flesh and bring me wine
Bring me pine logs hither
Thou and I shall see him dine
When we bear them thither.
Page and monarch, forth they went
Forth they went together
Through the rude winds wild lament
And the bitter weather

Sire, the night is darker now
And the wind blows stronger
Fails my heart, I know not how
I can go no longer.
Mark my footsteps, good my page
Tread thou in them boldly
Thou shall find the winters rage
Freeze thy blood less coldly.

In his masters step he trod
Where the snow lay dinted
Heat was in the very sod
Which the Saint had printed
Therefore, Christian men, be sure
Wealth or rank possessing
Ye, who now will bless the poor
Shall yourselves find blessing.

33. Hail Ye Flowers of Martyrs

All hail, ye little martyr flowers,
Sweet rosebuds cut in dawning hours!
When Herod sought the Christ to find
Ye fell as bloom before the wind.

First victims of the martyr bands,
With crowns and palms in tender hands,
Around the very altar, gay
And innocent, ye seem to play.

What profited this great offense?
What use was Herod's violence?
A Babe survives that dreadful day,
And Christ is safely borne away.

All honor, laud, and glory be,
O Jesus, virgin-born, to thee;
All glory, as is ever meet
Ao Father and to Paraclete.

34. Hark! The Herald Angels Sing

Hark! The herald angels sing
"Glory to the new-born king
Peace on earth and mercy mild
God and sinners reconciled"
Joyful all ye nations rise
Join the triumph of the skies
With angelic host proclaim
"Christ is born in Bethlehem"
Hark! The herald angels sing
"Glory to the new-born king"

Hail the heaven-born Prince of Peace!
Hail the Sun of Righteousness!
Light and life to all He brings
Risen with healing in His wings
Mild He lays His glory by

Born that man no more may die
Born to raise the sons of earth
Born to give them second birth
Hark! The herald angels sing
"Glory to the new-born king"

Hark! The herald angels sing
"Glory to the new-born king
Peace on earth and mercy mild
God and sinners reconciled"
Joyful all ye nations rise
Join the triumph of the skies
With angelic host proclaim
"Christ is born in Bethlehem"
Hark! The herald angels sing
"Glory to the new-born king"
"Glory to the new-born king"

35. Here We Come A-wassailing

Here we come a-wassailing
Among the leaves so green;
Here we come a-wand'ring
So fair to be seen.

(Chorus)
Love and joy come to you,
And to you your wassail too;
And God bless you
And send you a Happy New Year
And God send you a Happy New Year.

Our wassail cup is made
Of the rosemary tree,
And so is your beer
Of the best barley.

We are not daily beggars
That beg from door to door;
But we are neighbours' children,
Whom you have seen before.

Call up the butler of this house,
Put on his golden ring.
Let him bring us up a glass of beer,
And better we shall sing.

We have got a little purse
Of stretching leather skin;
We want a little of your money
To line it well within.

Bring us out a table
And spread it with a cloth;
Bring us out a mouldy cheese,
And some of your Christmas loaf.

God bless the master of this house
Likewise the mistress too,
And all the little children
That round the table go.

Good master and good mistress,
While you're sitting by the fire,
Pray think of us poor children
Who are wandering in the mire.

36.   I Heard the Bells on Christmas Day

I heard the bells on Christmas Day
Their old, familiar carols play,
And wild and sweet
The words repeat
Of peace on earth, good-will to men !

And thought how, as the day had come,
The belfries of all Christendom
Had rolled along

The unbroken song
Of peace on earth, good-will to men !

Till, ringing, singing on its way,
The world revolved from night to day
A voice, a chime,
A chant sublime
Of peace on earth, good-will to men !

Then from each black, accursed mouth,
The cannon thundered in the South,
And with the sound
The carols drowned
Of peace on earth, good-will to men !

It was as if an earthquake rent
The hearth-stones of a continent,
And made forlorn
The households born
Of peace on earth, good-will to men !

And in despair I bowed my head ;
"There is no peace on earth," I said ;
"For hate is strong
And mocks the song
Of peace on earth, good-will to men !"

Then pealed the bells more loud and deep:
"God is not dead ; nor doth he sleep !
The Wrong shall fail,

The Right prevail,
With peace on earth, good-will to men !"

37.   I Saw Three Ships (Come Sailing In)

I saw three ships come sailing in
On Christmas Day, on Christmas Day
I saw three ships come sailing in
On Christmas Day in the morning

And what was in those ships all three
On Christmas Day, on Christmas Day?
And what was in those ships all three
On Christmas Day in the morning?

Our Savior Christ and His lady
On Christmas Day, on Christmas Day
Our Savior Christ and His lady
On Christmas Day in the morning

Pray, wither sailed those ships all three
On Christmas Day, on Christmas Day
Pray, wither sailed those ships all three

On Christmas Day in the morning

O, they sailed into Bethlehem
On Christmas Day, on Christmas Day
O, they sailed into Bethlehem
On Christmas Day in the morning

And all the bells on Earth shall ring
On Christmas Day, on Christmas Day
And all the bells on Earth shall ring
On Christmas Day in the morning

38.   I Wonder as I Wander

I wonder as I wander out under the sky,
How Jesus the Savior did come for to die.
For poor on'ry people like you and like I...
I wonder as I wander out under the sky.

When Mary birthed Jesus 'twas in a cow's stall,
With wise men and farmers and shepherds and all.
But high from God's heaven a star's light did fall,
And the promise of ages it then did recall.

If Jesus had wanted for any wee thing,

A star in the sky, or a bird on the wing,
Or all of God's angels in heav'n for to sing,
He surely could have it, 'cause he was the King.

39. In the Bleak Midwinter

In the bleak mid-winter
Frosty wind made moan,
Earth stood hard as iron,
Water like a stone;
Snow had fallen, snow on snow,
Snow on snow,
In the bleak mid-winter
Long ago.

Our God, Heaven cannot hold Him
Nor earth sustain;
Heaven and earth shall flee away
When He comes to reign:
In the bleak mid-winter
A stable-place sufficed
The Lord God Almighty,
Jesus Christ.

Enough for Him, whom cherubim
Worship night and day,
A breastful of milk
And a mangerful of hay;
Enough for Him, whom angels
Fall down before,
The ox and ass and camel
Which adore.

Angels and archangels
May have gathered there,
Cherubim and seraphim
Thronged the air,
But only His mother
In her maiden bliss,
Worshipped the Beloved
With a kiss.

What can I give Him,
Poor as I am?
If I were a shepherd
I would bring a lamb,
If I were a wise man
I would do my part,
Yet what I can I give Him,
Give my heart.

40. Infant Holy, Infant Lowly

Infant holy, infant lowly,
for his bed a cattle stall;
oxen lowing, little knowing
Christ the babe is Lord of all.
Swiftly winging angels singing,
bells are ringing, tidings bringing:
Christ the child is Lord of all!
Christ the child is Lord of all!

Flocks were sleeping, shepherds keeping
vigil till the morning new
saw the glory, heard the story,
tidings of a gospel true.
Thus rejoicing, free from sorrow,
praises voicing, greet the morrow:
Christ the child was born for you!
Christ the child was born for you!

41. It Came Upon the Midnight Clear

It came upon the midnight clear,
That glorious song of old,
From angels bending near the earth,
To touch their harps of gold;
"Peace on the earth, good will to men,
From Heav'n's all-gracious King."
The world in solemn stillness lay,
To hear the angels sing.

Still through the cloven skies they come
With peaceful wings unfurled,
And still their heav'nly music floats
O'er all the weary world;
Above its sad and lowly plains,
They bend on hov'ring wing,
And ever o'er its Babel sounds
The blessed angels sing.

Yet with the woes of sin and strife
The world has suffered long;
Beneath the angel strain have rolled
Two thousand years of wrong;
And man, at war with man, hears not
The love-song which they bring;
Oh, hush the noise, ye men of strife
And hear the angels sing.

And ye, beneath life's crushing load,
Whose forms are bending low,
Who toil along the climbing way
With painful steps and slow,
Look now! for glad and golden hours
Come swiftly on the wing.
Oh, rest beside the weary road,
And hear the angels sing!

For lo! the days are hast'ning on,
By prophet seen of old,
When with the ever-circling years
Shall come the time foretold
When Christ shall come and all shall own
The Prince of Peace, their King,
And saints shall meet Him in the air,
And with the angels sing.

42. Jerusalem, Our Happy Home

Jerusalem, my happy home,
name ever dear to me!
when shall my sorrows have an end,
your joys when shall I see?

When shall I leave this dying world
and to that city rise;
when shall those mighty walls and gates
delight my wondering eyes?

That glorious hope, Jerusalem!
in faith I make my prayer:
O God, that all my grief might end,
O God, that I were there!

Apostles, martyrs, prophets, saints
around my saviour stand,
and all I love in Christ below
await his clear command.

Jerusalem, my happy home,
when shall that glory be
when all my labours have an end
and all your joys I see?

Lord Jesus Christ, prepare me now
for that dear home above;
to see, and know, and worship you
in your eternal love.

43. Jesus Christ the Apple Tree

The tree of life my soul hath seen
Laden with fruit, and always green:
The trees of nature fruitless be
Compared with Christ the apple tree

His beauty doth all things excel:
By faith I know, but ne'er can tell
The glory which I now can see
In Jesus Christ the apple tree

For happiness I long have sought
And pleasure dearly I have bought:
I missed of all; but now I see
'Tis found in Christ the apple tree

I'm weary with my former toil
Here I will sit and rest awhile:
Under the shadow I will be
Of Jesus Christ the apple tree

This fruit doth make my soul to thrive
It keeps my dying faith alive;
Which makes my soul in haste to be
With Jesus Christ the apple tree

44. Jingle Bells

Dashing through the snow
On a one horse open sleigh
O'er the fields we go,
Laughing all the way
Bells on bob tail ring,
making spirits bright
What fun it is to laugh and sing
A sleighing song tonight

Oh, jingle bells, jingle bells
Jingle all the way
Oh, what fun it is to ride
In a one horse open sleigh
Jingle bells, jingle bells
Jingle all the way
Oh, what fun it is to ride
In a one horse open sleigh

A day or two ago,
I thought I'd take a ride,
And soon Miss Fanny Bright
Was seated by my side;
The horse was lean and lank
Misfortune seemed his lot
We got into a drifted bank,
And then we got upsot.

Oh, jingle bells, jingle bells
Jingle all the way
Oh, what fun it is to ride
In a one horse open sleigh
Jingle bells, jingle bells
Jingle all the way
Oh, what fun it is to ride
In a one horse open sleigh

Jingle Bells, Jingle Bells,
Jingle all the way!
Oh, What fun it is to ride
In a one horse open sleigh.
Jingle Bells, Jingle Bells,
Jingle all the way!
Oh, What fun it is to ride
In a one horse open sleigh.

Now the ground is white
Go it while you're young
Take the girls tonight
And sing this sleighing song
Just get a bob tailed bay
two-forty as his speed
Hitch him to an open sleigh
And crack! you'll take the lead

Jingle Bells, Jingle Bells,
Jingle all the way!
Oh, What fun it is to ride
In a one horse open sleigh.
Jingle Bells, Jingle Bells,
Jingle all the way!
Oh, What fun it is to ride
In a one horse open sleigh.

45. Joy to the World

Joy to the world, the Lord is come
Let Earth receive her King
Let every heart prepare Him room
And Heaven and nature sing
And Heaven and nature sing
And Heaven, and Heaven, and nature sing

Joy to the Earth, the Savior reigns
Let all their songs employ
While fields and floods, rocks, hills and plains
Repeat the sounding joy
Repeat the sounding joy
Repeat, repeat, the sounding joy

He rules the world with truth and grace
And makes the nations prove
The glories of His righteousness
And wonders of His love
And wonders of His love
And wonders, wonders, of His love

Joy to the world, the Lord is come
Let Earth receive her King
Let every heart prepare Him room
And Heaven and nature sing
(And Heaven and nature sing)
And Heaven and nature sing
(And Heaven and nature sing)
And Heaven, and Heaven, and nature sing
And Heaven, and Heaven, and nature sing

Joy to the world, the Lord is come
Let Earth receive her King
Let every heart prepare Him room
And Heaven and nature sing
(And Heaven and nature sing)
And Heaven and nature sing
(And Heaven and nature sing)
And Heaven, and Heaven, and nature sing
And Heaven, and Heaven, and nature sing

46. Judea

A virgin unspotted, the prophet foretold
Should bring forth a Savior, which now we behold
To be our Redeemer from death, hell, and sin
Which Adam's transgression entangled us in

Then let us be merry, put sorrow away
Christ Jesus our Savior was born on this day

At Bethlehem city in Jewry it was
That Joseph and Mary together did pass
All for to be taxèd with many one moe
Great Caesar commanded the same should be so

Then let us be merry, put sorrow away
Christ Jesus our Savior was born on this day

But when they had entered the city so fair
A number of people so mighty was there
That Joseph and Mary, whose substance was small
Could find in the inn there no lodging at all

Then let us be merry, put sorrow away
Christ Jesus our Savior was born on this day

Then they were constrained in a stable to lie
Where horses and asses they used for to tie:

Their lodging so simple they took it no scorn
Before the next morning our Savior was born

47.   Little Donkey

Little donkey, little donkey
On the dusty road
Gotta keep on plodding onward
With your precious load

Been a long time little donkey
Through the winters night
Don't give up now little donkey
Bethlehem's in sight

Ring out those bells tonight
Bethlehem, Bethlehem
Follow that little star tonight
Bethlehem, Bethlehem

Little donkey, little donkey
Had a heavy day
Little donkey, carry Mary safely on her way
Little donkey, carry Mary safely on her-

Little donkey, little donkey
Journey's end is near
There's a guiding star up in the
Heaven shining clear
Little donkey, carry Mary safely on her way
Little donkey, carry Mary safely on her way

48. Love Came Down at Christmas

Love came down at Christmas
Love, a lovely love divine
Love was born at Christmas
Stars and angels gave the sign

Love will be our token
Love be yours, and love be mine
Love from God to all of us
Love for plea and gift a sign

Love for the 10 commandments
Love for the 9 that dress so fine
Love for the 8 that stood at the gate
Love for the 7 who went up to Heaven
Love for the 6 that never got fixed

Love for the 5 that stayed alive
Love for the 4 that stood at the door
Love for the Hebrew children
Love from the little babe, baby

49.   Mary's Boy Child

Long time ago in Bethlehem
So the Holy Bible say
Mary's boy child, Jesus Christ
Was born on Christmas Day.

Hark now hear the angels sing
A new king born today
And man will live for evermore
Because of Christmas Day.

While shepherds watched their flock by night,
They saw a bright new shining star
They hear a choir sing
The music seemed to come from afar.

Now Joseph, and his wife Mary,
Come to Bethlehem that night,
Them find no place to born she child,

Not a single room was in sight.

Hark, now hear the angels sing,
A new king born today,
And man will live for evermore,
Because of Christmas Day.

By and by them find a little nook
In a stable all forlorn,
And in a manger cold and dark,
Mary's little boy was born.

Hark now hear the angels sing,
A new king born today,
And man will live for evermore
Because of Christmas Day

50. Masters in this hall

Masters in this hall
Hear ye news today,
Brought from over seas
And ever you I pray:

[Chorus]
Sing we now noel,
Sing we noel clear!
Holpen all the folk on earth
Born the Son of God so dear!

Then to Bethl'em town
Went we two by two,
In a sorry place
We heard the oxen low:

Ox and ass Him know,
Kneeling on their knee,
Wonderous joy had I
This little babe to see

This is Christ, the Lord,
Masters be ye glad!
Christmas is come in,
And no folk shall be sad!

51. Silent night

Silent night! Holy night!
All is calm, all is bright
'round yon virgin mother and child!
Holy infant, so tender and mild,
sleep in heavenly peace,
sleep in heavenly peace.

Silent night! Holy night!
Shepherds quake at the sight.
Glories stream from heaven afar,
heav'nly hosts sing: "Alleluia!
Christ the Savior is born!
Christ the Savior is born!"

Silent night! Holy night!
Son of God, love's pure light
radiant beams from Thy holy face
with the dawn of redeeming grace,
Jesus, Lord, at Thy birth!
Jesus, Lord, at Thy birth!

Silent night! Holy night!
Wondrous star, lend thy light;
with the angels let us sing
"Alleluia" to our King:
"Christ the Savior is born!
Christ the Savior is born."

52. Now To Conclude Our Christmas Mirth

Now to conclude our Christmas mirth, With the news of our redemption,
we will end our songs on our Savour's birth, With the one that deserves attention.
Three great wonders fell on this day; a star brought Kings where the Infant lay,
Water made wine in Galilee, And Christ baptised in Jordan.

Those kings might have known what Balaam of old said of a star that would arise
In Jacob's land, when he foretold the coming of the Messias.
Jaspar, Melchior and Baltazar set out when they saw the new bright star,
Leaving their eastern kingdoms far to find out the new-born Jesus.

They steered their course to the Jewish court, Jerusalem renowned;
Where to find Him they did not doubt, but met with a stranger crowned.
The tyrant Herod shocked at the news to hear of a new-born King of the Jews,
In dread the usurped crown to lose, ordered a bloody

slaughter.

But for amends in this surprise those straying kings did visit
The Temple made by Solomon the Wise, the world had nothing like it.
Sapphires and gold there they could see, diamonds rich and ivory,
Embroidered silks and tapestry from both sides of the Indias.

Yet nothing rare or rich in art, not finding Him, could please them
They are told for Bethlehem to depart, no court toys could delay them.
Their guiding star again did appear and to the city straight did steer,
And over the stall resting most clear it bade the monarchs welcome.

Amazed to see the cottage poor, the stall where He was born,
They left their retinue at the door, though great, they entered without scorn;
The Blessed Babe and Mother found, laying their crowns and sceptres down,
Adored Him prostate on the ground and might have spoke as follows:

"O King of Kings herein disguise, Whom stars obey and

angels serve.
Though wealth and grandeur You despise, You have given us more than we deserve.
Our beds are gold and ivory, our garments netted with broidery,
Beset with pearls and pageantry, whilst You lie in a stable.

"Here's gold and myrrh and frankincense, not to enrich we bring,
But to honour Thee, O Heavenly Prince, as God and Man and King.
Incense to You as God is due, the gold shows kingly power too,
The myrrh keeps corpse long sweet and new; we have heard how You must suffer."

And when the grand affair is done, the world from Hell redeemed,
When God has glorified His Son, at length by men esteemed,
Let our poor pagan nations in, and to Thy happy sheep-fold bring,
That free from blindness and from sin, we may in truth adore You."

What else might have passed, you may conceive, in this fond conversation;
They bade farewell, taking their leave, home to their habitation.

Farewell good Christians, fare you well too, many Happy Christmases I wish you;
With a blessed end for to ensue, through the merits of Sweet Jesus.

53. In Dulci Jubilo

In dulci jubilo,*
nun singet und seid froh!
Unsers Herzens Wonne
leit in præsepio
und leuchtet als die Sonne
matris in gremio.
Alpha es et O.
O Jesu parvule,
nach dir ist mir so weh.
Tröst mir mein Gemüte,
o puer optime;
durch alle deine Güte,
o princeps gloriae,
trahe me post te.
Ubi sunt gaudia?
Nirgend mehr denn da,
da die Engel singen
nova cantica
und die Schellen klingen

in regis curia.
Eia, wärn wir da!
O pater caritas
o mater lenitas
wir waren gar verdorben
per nostra crimina:
So hast du uns erworben
coelorum gaudia.
Maria, hilf uns da!

54. O come, O come, Emmanuel

O come, O come, Emmanuel
And ransom captive Israel
That mourns in lonely exile here
Until the Son of God appear

Rejoice! Rejoice! Emmanuel
Shall come to thee, O Israel

O come, O come, Thou Lord of might
Who to Thy tribes, on Sinai's height
In ancient times didst give the law
In cloud, and majesty and awe

Rejoice! Rejoice! Emmanuel

Shall come to thee, O Israel

O come, Thou Rod of Jesse, free
Thine own from Satan's tyranny
From depths of hell Thy people save
And give them victory o'er the grave

55. O Holy Night

O Holy night! The stars are brightly shining
It is the night of our dear Savior's birth
Long lay the world in sin and error pining
'Til He appears and the soul felt its worth
A thrill of hope the weary world rejoices
For yonder breaks a new and glorious morn
Fall on your knees; O hear the Angel voices!
O night divine, O night when Christ was born
O night, O Holy night, O night divine!

Led by the light of Faith serenely beaming
With glowing hearts by His cradle we stand
So led by light of a star sweetly gleaming
Here come the Wise Men from Orient land
The King of kings lay thus in lowly manger
In all our trials born to be our friend

He knows our need, to our weakness is no stranger
Behold your King; before Him lowly bend
Behold your King; before Him lowly bend

Truly He taught us to love one another;
His law is love and His Gospel is Peace
Chains shall He break, for the slave is our brother
And in His name, all oppression shall cease
Sweet hymns of joy in grateful chorus raise we
Let all within us Praise His Holy name
Christ is the Lord; O praise His name forever!
His power and glory evermore proclaim
His power and glory evermore proclaim

56. O Little Town of Bethlehem

O little town of Bethlehem,
How still we see thee lie!
Above thy deep and dreamless sleep
The silent stars go by.
Yet in thy dark streets shineth
The everlasting Light;
The hopes and fears of all the years

Are met in thee to-night.

O morning stars, together
Proclaim the holy birth!
And praises sing to God the King,
And peace to men on earth.
For Christ is born of Mary
And gathered all above,
While mortals sleep the Angels keep
Their watch of wondering love.

How silently, how silently,
The wondrous gift is given;
So God imparts to human hearts
The blessings of His Heaven.
No ear may hear His coming,
But in this world of sin,
Where meek souls will receive Him still,
The dear Christ enters in.

Where children pure and happy
Pray to the blessed Child,
Where misery cries out to Thee,
Son of the Mother mild;1
Where Charity stands watching
And Faith holds wide the door,
The dark night wakes, the glory breaks,
And Christmas comes once more.

O holy Child of Bethlehem,
Descend to us, we pray!
Cast out our sin and enter in,
Be born in us to-day.
We hear the Christmas angels,
The great glad tidings tell;
O come to us, abide with us,
Our Lord Emmanuel!

57. Of the Father's Heart Begotten (Of the Father's Love Begotten)

Of the Father's heart begotten
Ere the world from chaos rose,
He is Alpha: from that Fountain,
All that is and hath been flows;
He is Omega, of all things
Yet to come the mystic Close,
Evermore and evermore.

By his word was all created;
He commanded and 'twas done;
Earth and sky and boundless ocean,
Universe of three in one,

All that sees the moon's soft radiance,
All that breathes beneath the sun,
Evermore and evermore.

He assumed this mortal body,
Frail and feeble, doomed to die,
That the race from dust created
Might not perish utterly,
Which the dreadful Law had sentenced
In the depths of hell to lie,
Evermore and evermore.

O how blest that wondrous birthday,
When the Maid the curse retrieved,
Brought to birth mankind's salvation,
By the Holy Ghost conceived,
And the Babe, the world's Redeemer,
In her loving arms received,
Evermore and evermore.

This is he, whom seer and sybil
Sang in ages long gone by;
This is he of old revealed
In the page of prophecy;
Lo! he comes, the promised Saviour;
Let the world his praises cry!
Evermore and evermore.

Sing, ye heights of heaven, his praises;
Angels and Archangels, sing!
Wheresoe'er ye be, ye faithful,
Let your joyous anthems ring,
Every tongue his name confessing,
Countless voices answering,
Evermore and evermore.

Hail! thou Judge of souls departed;
Hail! of all the living King!
On the Father's right hand throned,
Through his courts thy praises ring,
Till at lest for all offences
Righteous judgement thou shalt bring,
Evermore and evermore.

At the entrance into the Choir
Now let old and young uniting
Chant to thee harmonious lays
Maid and matron hymn thy glory,
Infant lips their anthem raise,
Boys and girls together singing
With pure heart their song of praise,
Evermore and evermore.

Let the storm and summer sunshine,
Gliding stream and sounding shore,
Sea and forest, frost and zephyr,

Day and night their Lord alone;
Let creation join to laud thee
Through the ages evermore,
Evermore and evermore. Amen.

58. Once in Royal David's City

Once in royal David's city
stood a lowly cattle shed,
where a mother laid her baby
in a manger for his bed:
Mary was that mother mild,
Jesus Christ, her little child.

He came down to earth from heaven
who is God and Lord of all,
and his shelter was a stable,
and his cradle was a stall;
with the poor and mean and lowly,
lived on earth our Savior holy.

And our eyes at last shall see him,
through his own redeeming love,
for that child, so dear and gentle,
is our Lord in heav'n above,

and he leads his children on
to the place where he is gone.

Not in that poor, lowly stable
with the oxen standing by
we shall see him, but in heaven,
set at God's right hand on high.
Then like stars his children crowned,
all in white, his praise will sound.

59. Past Three O'Clock (or Past Three a Clock)

Past three a clock,
And a cold frosty morning,
Past three a clock;
Good morrow, masters all!

Born is a Baby,
Gentle as may be,
Son of the eternal
Father supernal.

Past three a clock,
And a cold frosty morning,

Past three a clock;
Good morrow, masters all!

Seraph quire singeth,
Angel bell ringeth;
Hark how they rime it,
Time it and chime it.

Mid earth rejoices
Hearing such voices
e'ertofore so well
Carolling Nowell.

Hinds o'er the pearly,
Dewy lawn early
Seek the high Stranger
Laid in the manger.

Cheese from the dairy
Bring they for Mary
And, not for money,
Butter and honey.

Light out of star-land
Leadeth from far land
Princes, to meet him,
Worship and greet him.

Myrrh from full coffer,
Incense they offer;
Nor is the golden
Nugget withholden.

Thus they: I pray you,
Up, sirs, nor stay you
Till ye confess him
Likewise and bless him

60.   Rise Up Shepherd and Foller

There's a star in the East on Christmas morn;
Rise up, shepherd, and follow;
It will lead to the place where the Christ was born;
Rise up, shepherd, and follow.

Refrain:
Follow, follow;
Rise up, shepherd, and follow.
Follow the Star of Bethlehem;
Rise up, shepherd, and follow.

Leave your sheep, leave your sheep, and leave your lambs;
Rise up, shepherd, and follow;
Leave your ewes and your rams, leave your ewes and rams;
Rise up, shepherd, and follow.

If you take good heed to the angel's words;
Rise up, shepherd, and follow;
You'll forget your flocks, you'll forget your herds;
Rise up, shepherd, and follow.

61. Rudolph, the Red-Nosed Reindeer

You know Dasher and Dancer and Prancer and Vixen
Comet and Cupid and Donner and Blitzen
But do you recall
The most famous reindeer of all?

Rudolph the Red-Nosed Reindeer
Had a very shiny nose
And if you ever saw it
You would even say it glows

All of the other reindeer
Used to laugh and call him names
They never let poor Rudolph
Join in any reindeer games

Then one foggy Christmas Eve
Santa came to say
"Rudolph, with your nose so bright
Won't you guide my sleigh tonight?"

Then how the reindeer loved him
As they shouted out with glee
"Rudolph the Red-Nosed Reindeer
You'll go down in history"

Rudolph the Red-Nosed Reindeer
Had a very shiny nose
And if you ever saw it
You would even say it glows

All of the other reindeer
Used to laugh and call him names
They never let poor Rudolph
Join in any reindeer games

Then one foggy Christmas Eve
Santa came to say

"Rudolph, with your nose so bright
Won't you guide my sleigh tonight?"

Then how the reindeer loved him
As they shouted out with glee
"Rudolph the Red-Nosed Reindeer
You'll go down in history"

62.   Sans Day Carol

Now the holly bears a berry as white as the milk,
And Mary bore Jesus, all wrapped up in silk,
And Mary bore Jesus Christ our Saviour for to be,
And the first tree in the greenwood, it was the holly.
Holly! Holly!
And the first tree in the greenwood, it was the holly!

Now the holly bears a berry as green as the grass,
And Mary bore Jesus, who died on the cross,
And Mary bore Jesus Christ our Saviour for to be,
And the first tree in the greenwood, it was the holly.
Holly! Holly!

And the first tree in the greenwood, it was the holly!

Now the holly bears a berry as black as the coal,
And Mary bore Jesus, who died for us all,
And Mary bore Jesus Christ our Saviour for to be,
And the first tree in the greenwood, it was the holly.
Holly! Holly!
And the first tree in the greenwood, it was the holly!

Now the holly bears a berry as blood is it red,
And Mary bore Jesus who rose from the dead,
And Mary bore Jesus Christ our Saviour for to be,
And the first tree in the greenwood, it was the holly.
Holly! Holly!
And the first tree in the greenwood, it was the holly!

63. See, amid the Winter's Snow

See amid the winter's snow,
Born for us on earth below,
See the tender Lamb appears,
Promised from eternal years.

Chorus
Hail, thou ever-blessed morn!
Hail, redemption's happy dawn!
Sing through all Jerusalem,
Christ is born in Bethlehem.

Lo, within a manger lies
He who built the starry skies;
He, who throned in height sublime
Sits amid the cherubim. Chorus

Say, ye holy shepherds, say
What your joyful news today;
Wherefore have ye left your sheep
On the lonely mountain steep? Chorus

"As we watched at dead of night,
Lo, we saw a wondrous light;1
Angels singing peace on earth
Told us of the Saviour's birth". Chorus

Sacred infant, all divine,
What a tender love was Thine,
Thus to come from highest bliss
Down to such a world as this. Chorus

Teach, O teach us , Holy Child,
By Thy Face so meek and mild,

Teach us to resemble Thee,
In Thy Sweet humility! Chorus

64. Shepherds Arise

Shepherds arise be not afraid,
with hasty steps repair
to David's city, sing sing all earth,
with our blest infant there,
with our blest infant there,
with our blest infant there.

Chorus
Sing, sing all earth,
sing, sing all earth,
eternal praises sing to our redeemer,
to our redeemer and our heav'nly king.

Laid in a manger view a child,
humility divine,
sweet innocence sounds meek and mild,
grace in his features shine,
grace in his features shine,
grace in his features shine.

65. Silver Bells

City sidewalks, busy sidewalks.
Dressed in holiday style
In the air
There's a feeling
of Christmas
Children laughing
People passing
Meeting smile after smile
and on every street corner you'll hear

Silver bells, silver bells
It's Christmas time in the city
Ring-a-ling, hear them sing
Soon it will be Christmas day

66. Sir Chrìstemas

Nowell, nowell, nowell, nowell
Who is there that singeth so nowell, nowell, nowell?

I am here, Sir Chrìstëmas
Welcome, my lord Sir Chrìstëmas
Welcome to us all, both more and less

Come near, nowell

Dieus wous garde, bewe sieurs, tidings I you bring:
A maid hath borne a child full ying
The which causeth you for to sing
Nowell

Christ is now born of a pure maid
In an ox-stall he is laid
Whereof sing we alle at a brayde
Nowell

Bevvex bien par tutte la company
Make good cheer and be right merry
And sing with us now joyfully
Nowell

67. St John did Lean on Jesus' Breast

Saint John did lean on Jesus's breast,
Jesus loved John more than the rest,
Our loving Jesus St. John did love,
His Gospel doth it clearly prove;
Then let St. John be loved by us,

Who was beloved by our Jesus.

Divine mysteries locked under seal
To St. John Jesus did reveal,
His secrets did to him impart,
Made him the treasurer of His heart;
Then let St. John be loved by us,
Who was beloved by our Jesus.

He was disciple, evangelist,
Apostle, prophet, what he list;
To him, His most darling friend
Jesus His mother did commend;
Then let St. John be loved by us,
Who was beloved by our Jesus.

68. Star of the East

Star of the East, Oh Bethlehem's star,
Guiding us on to Heaven afar!
Sorrow and grief and lull'd by thy light,
Thou hope of each mortal, in death's lonely night!

Fearless and tranquil, we look up to Thee!

Knowing thou beam'st thro' eternity!
Help us to follow where Thou still dost guide,
Pilgrims of earth so wide.

Star of the East, thou hope of the soul,
While round us here the dark billows roll,
Lead us from sin to glory afar,
Thou star of the East, thou sweet Bethlehem's star.

Star of the East, un-dim'd by each cloud,
What tho' the storms of grief gather loud?
Faithful and pure thy rays beam to save,
Still bright o'er the cradle, and bright o'er the grave!

Smiles of a Saviour are mirror'd in Thee!
Glimpses of Heav'n in thy light we see!
Guide us still onward to that blessed shore,
After earth's toil is o'er!

Star of the East, thou hope of the soul,
While round us here the dark billows roll,
Lead us from sin to glory afar,
Thou star of the East, thou sweet Bethlehem's star.

Oh star that leads to God above!
Whose rays are peace and joy and love!
Watch o'er us still till life hath ceased,
Beam on, bright star, sweet Bethlehem star

69. Sweet Jesus Was the Sacred Name

Sweet Jesus was the sacred name
Of the sweet Babe who to us came,
Angels and men this Name adore
Both now and then and evermore;
A saving Name, this Saviour He
Doth save us for eternity.

Good God, how precious is this Name!
He gave His blood to gain the same;
To honour it all knees bow down
In heaven and earth and underground;
And every tongue confess that He
Doth save us for eternity.

Then. Jesus I adore Thy Name,
And ever shall adore the same,
Thy Name be graven on my heart,
Live always there and ne'er depart;
My prayers day and night shall be,
Save us Jesus, Jesus save me.

70. Sweet Little Jesus Boy

Sweet little Jesus Boy
They made You be born in a manguh
Sweet little Holy chil'
Didn't know who You wus.

Didn't know You'd come to save us Lawd
To take our sins away.
Our eyes wus bline;
We couldn't see
We didn't know who You wus.

Long time ago You wus bawn
Bawn in a manguh low,
Sweet little Jesus Boy.
De worl' treat You mean Lawd,
Treat me mean too.
But please, Suh, fuhgive us Lawd;
We didn't know 'twas You.

Sweet little Jesus Boy
Bawn long time ago,
Sweet little Holy chil'
An' we didn't know who You wus.

71. Sweetest of All Names, Jesus

Sweetest of all names, Jesus,
Bless this New Year's Day for us;
Grant new hearts, then all is new,
The year, Thy Name, Thy people too.

Thy Name is sweeter than all (gain),
Cheap though purchased with much pain,
Richer than the monarch's crown;
Not all the world worth it alone.

Nothing dearer can we bring,
Nothing sweeter can we sing;
Tongue can't express—thoughts fails us
To comprehend our dear Jesus.

(Mercy) to all that will amend;
(Thankful for every good intent;
(To him) who seeks, sweets to excess,
(In Jesus) such as do possess.

deceitful hearts
sharping arts,
honest hear alone,
Jesus dwells as on a rich throne.

(Come then) Sweet Saviour, take Thy place,
(Though we have sinned), this once release;
(Alone) Thy Name, Sweet Jesus,

Is dearer than the world to us.

Nature's laws to Him gave way,
And all her rules must Him obey;
A Virgin pure doth Him conceive,
the grave.

From Hell He frees the souls of men,
Who those four thousand years (had been)
The princes of the Blessed abode
Lift up their gates and clear the . . . .

He triumphed over death and Hell;
His wonders all no man can tell;
The dead He raised, He cured the blind,
He healed the sick of every kind.

The world He ransomed by His death;
The world He conquered by His Life;
A poor Man humble crucified
Did more than Cæsar with his . . . .

Lovely Jesus, I adore Thee,
In all shapes and every form,
An Infant as the Virgin bore Thee,
As well as on Thy shining throne.

Every knee to Thee shall bend,
Every tongue shall Thee commend,
Every heart shall Thee love;
May this New Year happy prove.

(Let not) this year, as past we've done
(Be) without thoughts of going home,
We're strangers here, our port is Heaven,
The storms are great, steer stead~' then.

When the hour calls us away,
Oh, grant, Sweet Jesus that we may
(In virtue) of this costly Name
(Enter Life) without sin or stain.

72. The Angel Said to Joseph Mild

The angel saith to Joseph mild,
Fly with the Mother and the Child,
Out of this land to Egypt go,
Our heavenly Babe will have it so;
For that His hour is not yet come
To die for man's redemption.

Proud Herod, he doth froth and frown,
Feareth to loose kingdom and crown;
Full of disdain and full of scorn~
He must destroy this young King born;
But stay, His hour is not yet come

To die for man's redemption.

Herod, forbear this cruel flood
Of the most pure innocent blood,
To thee a crown this Child doth bring
To make thee happier than a king;
From highest heavens along He's come
To die for man's redemption.

73. The Babe in Bethlem's Manger

The Babe in Bethl'em's manger laid,
In humble form so low,
By wond'ring angels is surveyed
Through all His scenes of woe.

Refrain:
Noël, Noël,
Now sing a Savior's birth,
All hail His coming down to earth,
Who raises us to heav'n.

A Savior, sinners all around!
Sing, shout the wondrous word;

Let every bosom hail the sound,
A Savior! Christ the Lord.

For, not to sit on David's throne
With worldly pomp and joy,
He came for sinners to atone,
And Satan to destroy.

Well may we sing the Savior's birth,
Who need the grace so given,
And hail His coming down to earth,
Who raises us to heaven.

74. The Cherry-Tree Carol

When Joseph was an old man, an old man was he
He married Virgin Mary, the queen of Galilee
He married Virgin Mary, the queen of Galilee

Joseph and Mary walked through an orchard green
There were berries and cherries, as thick as might be seen
There were berries and cherries, as thick as might be seen

And Mary spoke to Joseph, so meek and so mild
"Joseph, gather me some cherries for I am with child"

"Joseph, gather me some cherries for I am with child"

And Joseph flew in anger, in anger flew he
"Let the father of the baby gather cherries for thee"
"Let the father of the baby gather cherries for thee"

Then up spoke baby Jesus, from in Mary's womb
"Bend down the tallest tree that my mother might have some"
"Bend down the tallest tree that my mother might have some"

And bend down the tallest branch till it touched Mary's hand
Cried she, "Oh, look thou Joseph, I have cherries by command"
Cried she, "Oh, look thou Joseph, I have cherries by command"

75. The Darkest Midnight in December

The darkest midnight in December,
No snow, no hail, nor winter storm,
Shall hinder us for to remember,
The Babe that on this night was born.

With shepherds we are come to see,
This lovely Infants glorious charms,
Born of a maid as prophets said,
The God of love in Mary's arms.

No earthly gifts can we present Him,
No gold nor myrrh nor odours sweet.
But if with hearts we can content Him
We humbly lay them at his feet.
'Twas but pure love that from above
Brought Him to save us from all harms
So let us sing and welcome Him,
The God of Love in Mary's arms.

Four thousand years from the creation
The world lay groaning under sin
No one could e'er expect salvation
No one could enter Heaven.
'Twas Adam's fall had damned us all
To Hell, to endless pains forlorn:
'Twas so decreed we'd have ne'er been freed,
Had not this heavenly Babe been born.

But here the best of heads will grumble,
The faithless Jews will not adore
A God so poor, so mean, so humble,
A child they scorn to kneel before.
But, oh, give ear, and you shall hear
How all those wonders came to pass;

Why Christ was born to suffer scorn,
And lodged between an ox and ass.

Have you not heard the sacred story,
How man was made those seats to fill,
Which the fallen angels lost in glory
By their presumption, pride and will?
They thought us mean for to obtain
Such glorious seats and crowns in heaven,
So through a cheat they got Eve to eat
The fruit, to be avenged on man.

Thus we were lost, our God offended,
The devils triumphing in our shame.
What recompense could be pretended?
No man could ever wipe off the stain.
Till God alone from His high throne
Becoming Man did us restore
Let us rejoice in tuneful voice,
Let Satan tremble and adore,

If by a woman we were wounded.
Another woman brings the cure;
If by a fruit we were confounded.
A tree our safety would procure.
They laughed at man, but if they can
Let Satan with his hellish swarms
Refuse to kneel and honour yield
To the lovely Babe in Mary's arms.

We like beasts lay in a stable,
Our senses blind and dead by sin
To help ourselves we not able,
But He brings grace and life again.
Thus conquered hell, confined the devil,
To free our souls from endless harms
His life He gave and now you have
The God of Love in Mary's arms.

Ye faithful hearts be not offended
To own your God though seeming mean
By this from Hell you were defended,
Your joys were purchased by His pain.
The Lord of all comes to a stall,
And to attend Him sends for Kings
Who by a star are called from far,
To see and hear those joyful things.

Oh, God! although man did offend Thee,
Here is a Man that must Thee please;
Though to compassion none could bend Thee,
Thy anger now must surely cease.
And when our crimes in aftertimes
May Thee to anger justly move,
Pray grant us peace, seeing the face
Of this Thy Son and God of Love.

Ye blessed angels join our voices
Let your gilded wings beat fluttering over,

Whilst every st~til set free rejoices,
And every devil must adore.
We'll sing and pray that He always may
Our Church and clergyman defend,
God grant us grace in all our days,
A merry Christmas and a happy end.

76. The First Noel (The First Nowell)

The First Noel the angel did say
Was to certain poor shepherds
in fields as they lay;
In fields as they lay, keeping their sheep,
On a cold winter's night that was so deep.

Noel, Noel, Noel, Noel,
Born is the King of Israel.

They looked up and saw a star
Shining in the east beyond them far,
And to the earth it gave great light,
And so it continued both day and night.

And by the light of that same star
Three wise men came from country far;

To seek for a king was their intent,
And to follow the star wherever it went.

This star drew nigh to the northwest,
O'er Bethlehem it took it rest,
And there it did both stop and stay
Right over the place where Jesus lay.

Then entered in those wise men three
Full reverently upon their knee,
and offered there in his presence
Their gold, and myrrh, and frankincense.

Then let us all with one accord
Sing praises to our heavenly Lord;
That hath made heaven and earth of naught,
And with his blood mankind hath bought

77. The Friendly Beasts

Jesus our brother kind and good,
Was humbly born in a stable rude.
The friendly beasts around him stood.
Jesus our brother kind and good.

A brilliant star shone through the night
And filled the world with wondrous light
While friendly beasts stayed by his side
A brilliant star shone through the night

"I," Said the donkey, all shaggy and brown.
"I carried His mother uphill and down.
I carried her safely to Bethlehem town."
"I," Said the donkey all shaggy and brown.

"I," Said the cow, all white and red.
"I gave Him my manger, for a bed.
I gave Him my hay to pillow His head."
"I," Said the cow, all white and red.

"I," Said the sheep with the curly horn
I gave Him my wool for a blanket warm.
He wore my coat on Christmas morn."
"I," Said the sheep with the curly horn.

"I," Said the dove from the rafters high.
I cooed him to sleep so he wouldn't cry.
We cooed him to sleep my mate and I."
"I," Said the dove from the rafters high.

Every beast by some good spell
In the stable dark was glad to tell

Of the gifts they gave Emanuel.
The gifts they gave Emanuel.

78. The Holly and the Ivy

The holly and the ivy,
When they are both full grown,
Of all trees that are in the wood,
The holly bears the crown

O, the rising of the sun,
And the running of the deer
The playing of the merry organ,

The holly bears a blossom,
As white as lily flow'r,
And Mary bore sweet Jesus Christ,
To be our dear Saviour

O, the rising of the sun,
And the running of the deer
The playing of the merry organ,

The holly bears a berry,

As red as any blood,
And Mary bore sweet Jesus Christ,
To do poor sinners good

O, the rising of the sun,
And the running of the deer
The playing of the merry organ,

The holly bears a prickle,
As sharp as any thorn,
And Mary bore sweet Jesus Christ,
On Christmas Day in the morn

O, the rising of the sun,
And the running of the deer
The playing of the merry organ,

The holly bears a bark,
As bitter as the gall,
And Mary bore sweet Jesus Christ,
For to redeem us all

O, the rising of the sun,
And the running of the deer
The playing of the merry organ,

The holly and the ivy,
When they are both full grown,

Of all trees that are in the wood,
The holly bears the crown

O, the rising of the sun,
And the running of the deer
The playing of the merry organ,

79. The Little Drummer Boy

Come thy told me
Pa rum pum pum-pum
A newborn King to see
Pa rum pum pum-pum

Our finest gifts we bring
Pa rum pum pum-pum
To lay before the king
Pa rum pum pum-pum
Rum pum pum-pum Rum pum pum-pum

So to honor Him
Pa rum pum pum-pum

When we come

Little baby
Pa rum pum pum-pum
I am a poor boy too
Pa rum pum pum-pum

I have no gift to bring
Pa rum pum pum-pum
That's fit to give our King
Pa rum pum pum-pum
Rum pum pum-pum Rum pum pum-pum

Shall I play for you
Pa rum pum pum-pum
On my drum

Mary nodded
Pa rum pum pum-pum
The ox and lamb kept time
Pa rum pum pum-pum

I played my drum for Him
Pa rum pum pum-pum
I played my best for Him
Pa rum pum pum-pum
Rum pum pum-pum Rum pum pum-pum

Then He smiled at me
Pa rum pum pum-pum
Me and my drum

80. The Lord at first did Adam make

The Lord at first did Adam make
Out of the dust and clay,
And in his nostrils breathèd life,
E'en as the Scriptures say.
And then in Eden's paradise He placèd him to dwell,
That he within it should remain,
To dress and keep it well:

[Refrain]
Now let good Christians all begin
An holy life to live,
And to rejoice and merry be,
For this is Christmas Eve.

Now mark the goodness of the Lord,
Which he for mankind bore;
His mercy soon he did extend,
Lost man for to restore;

And then, for to redeem our souls
From death and hellish thrall,
He said his own dear Son should be
The Saviour of us all:

Now for the blessings we enjoy,
Which are from heaven above,
Let us renounce all wickedness,
And live in perfect love:
Then we shall do Christ's own command,
E'en his own written word;
And when we die, in heaven shall
Enjoy our living Lord:

And now the tide is nigh at hand,
In which our Saviour came;
Let us rejoice and merry be
In keeping of the same;
Let's feed the poor and hungry souls,
And such as do it crave;
And when we die, in heaven we
Our sure reward shall have:

81. The Rocking Carol

Little Jesus, sweetly sleep, do not stir;
We will lend a coat of fur,
We will rock you, rock you, rock you,
We will rock you, rock you, rock you:
See the fur to keep you warm,
Snugly round your tiny form.

Mary's little baby, sleep, sweetly sleep,
Sleep in comfort, slumber deep;
We will rock you, rock you, rock you,
We will rock you, rock you, rock you:
We will serve you all we can,
Darling, darling little man.

82. The Seven Joys of Mary

The very first joy that Mary had,
It was the joy of one
To see her blessed Jesus
When He was first her Son
When He was first her Son.

Chorus
When He was Her first Son, Good Lord;
And happy may we be,
Praise Father, Son, and Holy Ghost
To all eternity

The next good joy that Mary had,
It was the joy of two
To see her own son Jesus,
To make the lame to go.
To make the lame to go.

The next good joy that Mary had,
It was the joy of three
To see her own son Jesus,
To make the blind to see.
To make the blind to see.

The next good joy that Mary had,
It was the joy of four
To see her own son Jesus,
To read the Bible o'er.
To read the Bible o'er.

The next good joy that Mary had,
It was the joy of five
To see her own son Jesus,
To bring the dead alive.
To bring the dead alive.

The next good joy that Mary had,
It was the joy of six
To see her own son Jesus,
Upon the Crucifix.
Upon the Crucifix.

The next good joy that Mary had,
It was the joy of seven
To see her own son Jesus,
To wear the crown of Heaven
To wear the crown of Heaven

83.   There Is No Rose

There is no rose of such virtue
As is the rose that bare Jesu;
Alleluia.

There is no rose of such virtue
As is the rose that bare Jesu;
Alleluia.

For in this rose contained was
Heaven and earth in little space;
Res miranda.

By that rose we may well see
That he is God in persons three,
Pari forma.

The angels sungen the shepherds to:
Gloria in excelsis deo:
Gaudeamus.

Leave we all this worldly mirth,
And follow we this joyful birth;
Transeamus.

Alleluia, res miranda,
Pares forma, gaudeamus,
Transeamus.

84.   This Endris Night

This endris night I saw a sight,
A star as bright as day,
And ev'r among, a maiden sung,
"Lully, bye bye, lullay."

This lovely lady sat and sang,
And to her child did say,
"My son, my brother, father dear,
Why liest thou thus in hay?"

"My sweetest bird, 'tis thus required,
Though I be king veray,
But nevertheless I will not cease
To sing 'Bye bye, lullay.'"

The child then spake in his talking,
And to his mother did say,
"Yea, I am known as heaven-king
In crib though I be laid.

"For angels bright down on me light;
Thou knowest 'tis no nay.
And for that sight thou may delight
To sing, 'Bye bye, lullay.'"

"Now, sweet son, since thou art a king,
Why art thou laid in stall?
Why dost not order thy bedding
In some great kinges hall?

"Methinks 'tis right that king or knight
Should lie in good array.
And then among, it were no wrong
To sing 'Bye bye, lullay.'"

"Mary mother, I am thy Child,
Though I be laid in stall;
For lords and dukes shall worship Me,
And so shall kingès all.

"Ye shall well see that kingès three

Shall come on this twelfth day.
For this behest give Me thy breast
And sing, By by, lullay."

"Now tell, sweet Son, I Thee do pray,
Thou art my Love and Dear—
How should I keep Thee to Thy pay,
And make Thee glad of cheer?

"For all Thy will I would fulfill—
Thou knowest well, in fay;
And for all this I will Thee kiss,
And sing, By by, lullay."

"My dear mother, when time it be,
Take thou Me up on loft,
And set Me then upon thy knee,
And handle me full soft.

"And in thy arm thou hold Me warm,
And keep Me night and day,
And if I weep, and may not sleep,
Thou sing, By by, lullay."

"Now sweet Son, since it is come so,
That all is at Thy will,
I pray Thee grant to me a boon,
If it be right and skill,—

"That child or man, who will or can
Be merry on my day,

To bliss Thou bring—and I shall sing,
Lullay, by by, lullay."

85. This is St Stephen's Day

This is St. Stephen's day, his feast we solemnize,
From him we learn to pardon and love our enemies.
He's the first Christian martyr who passed from earth to heaven,
By suffering hate and envy and injuries of men.

More just than the just Abel, this prince of martyrs died,
His blood not for revenge but for God's pardon cried;
For fury and for rage he did remission crave,
For malice he had mercy and love for hate he gave.

This soldier of the Cross, armed not with iron but faith,
Doth not assault but suffer all that man doth or saith;
On bended knees with hands and eyes fixed on the skies,
With humble heart he prays for murdering enemies.

He closed not up his lips whilst he enjoyed his breath
To gain for them a pardon who did procure his death;
Pardon, good God, their rage, this holy saint doth pray,
Lay not unto their charge whate'er they do or say.

This champion of the Cross to conquer death doth die,
Sufferings are his triumphs, death is his victory;
The stones like showers of hail, the Jews on him did cast,
Become pure crowns of pearls and palms which ever last.

He saw the heavens all open, his throne of glory drest,
His Saviour Christ prepared to place his soul in rest.
Then let us daily pray for those who us offend,
That with St. Stephen we may enjoy a blessed end.

86.   To Greet Our Saviour's Dear

To greet our Saviour's dear one I will give you a new song,
In honour of the great evangelist, St John,
To whom, Our Saviour dying, His Mother did commend,
And then made him her son who was His dearest friend.

Of John seek no parentage of nobleness or birth,
Since he has got a Brother, the King of Heaven and Earth.
For though he was a fisherman, taught to the nets and oar,
He is now the son of Mary, and who could wish for more.

But ye that are so curious his father for to know:
He is the son of thunder as Christ Himself doth show.
He is the towering eagle which serves the Mighty Jove
To spread his heavenly lightning and burn all hearts with

love.

To Christ we are all brothers by grace 'tis plain and clear,
But John among the rest is Benjamin the dear.
Not one besides His brother, search both earth and heaven,
Was so beloved by Jesus, by angels and by men.

Why then should we compare him to any of the rest,
Who was the loved disciple that leaned on Jesus' breast,
Where he sucked in such mysteries as ne'er till then were known
To angels or to prophets or man but John alone.

Our Church, the Spouse of Christ, was left to Peter's charge,
Though John had greater merit, he was not come of age,
Being as yet but twenty, he is fit to be a son,
But a husband to the Church, you see he is too young.

You have heard the love of Jesus and now hear that of John,
Who still stood by His Master when all the rest were gone,
Though Peter thrice denied Him before the cock did crow,
St. John loyal and constant unto the Cross did go.

The most afflicted Mother he lovingly did hand,
Arid whilst Our Saviour suffered along with her did stand.
When Christ said to the Virgin: "Woman, there is thy son,"
He said: "Look to thy Mother," unto His dear St. John.

No heart can here conceive nor any tongue express
Their tears, their grief, their fondness, their love and their distress,

All three were so united in that one dying Heart
Though two were forced to live they'd rather die than part.

In short when all was over—I will not raise your grief,
In this great time of joy, solemnlty, relief—
For fifteen years he served her as the most humble slave,
Until with his own hands he laid her in the grave.

When John had thus discharged his chief and only care,
He then begins to travel and preach both far and near.
If all his works and wonders to sing we did pretend,
A day would not suffice us, our song would never end.

Inflamed with Peter's glory, and Paul's, he goes to Rome,
Hoping as well as they to die by martyrdom.
He entered with great joy unto the tub of oil,
In which the cruel tyrants intended him to boil.

When this and all the rest of tortures they could invent
Could not molest or hurt him, he's doomed to banishment
Unto the Isle of Patmos with grief to end his days,
But he converts the people and leaves them long in peace.

To see the Church well grounded he's left till very old,
But the glad hour at length an angel him foretold,
His blood no hands of tyrant would God permit to stain,
But as he lived a Phoenix, he died by God's sweet flame.

His testament and will and constant theme before,
Was still "Love one another" be said it o'er and o'er
Thus peacefully he died, the earth could not contain

His virgin corpse which angels triumphing took to Heaven.

And now the loved disciple, amidst eternal bliss,
With Jesus and His Mother, he dwells in happiness
By Stephen we are taught to pardon, by John we are taught to love;
By following their example you'll rest with them above.

87. Torches

Torches, torches, run with torches
All the way to Bethlehem!
Christ is born and now lies sleeping;
Come and sing your song to Him!
Torches, torches, run with torches
All the way to Bethlehem!
Christ is born and now lies sleeping;
Come and sing your song to Him!

Ah, Roro, Roro, my baby
Ah, Roro, my love, Roro;
Sleep you well, my heart's own darling
While we sing you our Rorro

Sing, my friends, and make you merry
Joy and mirth and joy again;
Lo, He lives, the King of heaven
Now and evermore. Amen

Lo, He lives, the King of heaven
Now and ever, evermore. Amen

88. Unto Us a Boy is Born (Unto Us is Born a Son)

Unto us a boy is born!
The King of all creation,
Came he to a world forlorn,
The Lord of ev'ry nation.

Cradled in a stall was he
With sleepy cows and asses;
But the very beasts could see
That he the world surpasses.

Herod then with fear was filled:
"A prince," he said, "in Jewry!"

And all the little boys he killed
At Bethl'hem in his fury.

Now may Mary's son, who came
So long ago to love us,
Lead us all with hearts aflame
Unto the joys above us.

Alpha and Omega he!
Now let the organ thunder,
While the choir with peals of glee
Shall rend the air asunder.

89. We Three Kings of Orient Are

We three kings of Orient are;
bearing gifts we traverse afar,
field and fountain, moor and mountain,
following yonder star.

Refrain:
O star of wonder, star of light,
star with royal beauty bright,
westward leading, still proceeding,

guide us to thy perfect light.

Born a King on Bethlehem's plain,
gold I bring to crown him again,
King forever, ceasing never,
over us all to reign.

Frankincense to offer have I;
incense owns a Deity nigh;
prayer and praising, voices raising,
worshiping God on high.

Myrrh is mine; its bitter perfume
breathes a life of gathering gloom;
sorrowing, sighing, bleeding, dying,
sealed in the stone-cold tomb.

Glorious now behold him arise;
King and God and sacrifice:
Alleluia, Alleluia,
sounds through the earth and skies.

90. Wexford Carol

Good people all, this Christmas time
Consider well and bear in mind
What our good God for us has done
In sending His beloved Son

With Mary holy we should pray
To God with love this Christmas day
In Bethlehem upon that morn
There was a blessed Messiah born

Near Bethlehem did shepherds keep
Their flocks of lambs and feeding sheep
To whom God's angels did appear
Which put the shepherds in great fear

"Prepare to go, " the angels said
"To Bethlehem, be not afraid
For there you'll find this happy morn
A princely Babe, sweet Jesus born"

With thankful heart and joyful mind
The shepherds went the Babe to find
And as God's angel had foretold
They did our Saviour Christ behold

Within a manger He was laid
And by his side the Virgin maid
As long foretold upon that morn
There was a blessed Messiah born

91. What Child Is This?

What child is this, who, laid to rest,
On Mary's lap is sleeping,
Whom angels greet with anthems sweet
While shepherds watch are keeping?
This, this is Christ the King,
Whom shepherds guard and angels sing;
Haste, haste to bring Him laud,
The babe, the son of Mary!

Why lies He in such mean estate
Where ox and ass are feeding?
Good Christian, fear: for sinners here
The silent Word is pleading.
Nails, spear shall pierce him through,
The Cross be borne for me, for you;
Hail, hail the Word Made Flesh,

The babe, the son of Mary!

So bring Him incense, gold, and myrrh;
Come, peasant, king, to own Him!
The King of Kings salvation brings;
Let loving hearts enthrone Him!
Raise, raise the song on high!
The virgin sings her lullaby.
Joy! joy! for Christ is born,
The babe, the son of Mary!

92. Whence Is That Lovely Fragrance

Whence is the goodly fragrance flowing,
Stealing our senses all away,
never the like did come a-blowing,
Shepherds, in flow'ry fields of May,
Whence is that goodly fragrance flowing,
Stealing our senses all away.

What is that light so brilliant, breaking
Here in the night across our eyes.
Never so bright, the day-star waking,
Started to climb the morning skies!

What is that light so brilliant, breaking,
Here in the night across our eyes.

Bethlehem! there in manger lying,
Find your Redeemer haste away,
Run ye with eager footsteps vieing!
Worship the Saviour born today.
Bethlehem! there in manger lying,
Find your Redeemer haste away.

93. While by My Sheep I Watched at Night

While by the sheep I watched at night,
glad tidings brought an angel bright.

Refrain:
How great our joy!
Great our joy!
Joy, joy, joy!
Joy, joy, joy!
Praise we the Lord in heaven on high!
Praise we the Lord in heaven on high!

There shall be born, so he did say,

in Bethlehem a child today.

There shall the child lie in a stall,
this child who shall redeem us all.

This gift of God we'll cherish well,
that ever joy our hearts shall fill.

94. While Shepherds Watched Their Flocks

While shepherds watched their flocks by night,
all seated on the ground,
an angel of the Lord came down,
and glory shone around.

"Fear not," said he for mighty dread
had seized their troubled mind
"glad tidings of great joy I bring
to you and all mankind.

"To you, in David's town, this day
is born of David's line
a Savior, who is Christ the Lord;

and this shall be the sign:

"The heavenly babe you there shall find
to human view displayed,
all simply wrapped in swaddling clothes
and in a manger laid."

Thus spoke the angel. Suddenly
appeared a shining throng
of angels praising God, who thus
addressed their joyful song:

"All glory be to God on high,
and to the earth be peace;
to those on whom his favor rests
goodwill shall never cease."

95. With Wondering Awe, the Wisemen Saw...

With wondering awe the wise men saw
The star in heaven springing,
And with delight, in peaceful night,
They heard the angel singing:

Hosanna, hosanna, hosanna to His name!

By light of star they traveled far
To seek the lowly manger,
A humble bed wherein was laid
The wondrous little Stranger.
Hosanna, hosanna, hosanna to His name!

And still is found, the world around,
The old and hallowed story,
And still is sung in every tongue
The angels' song of glory:
Hosanna, hosanna, hosanna to His name!

The heavenly star its rays afar
On every land is throwing,
And shall not cease till holy peace
In all the earth is growing.
Hosanna, hosanna, hosanna to His name!

96. Ye Sons of Men with Me Rejoice

Ye sons of men with me rejoice,
And praise the Heav'ns with heart and voice,

For joyful tidings you we bring,
Of this Heav'nly Babe, the new born King.

Who from His mighty throne above
Came down to manifest His love
To all such as would Him embrace,
And would be born again in grace.

The mystery for to unfold:
When the King of Kings He did behold
The poor unhappy state of man,,
He sent His dear beloved Son.

From the brink of Hell He set us free:
A greater love could never be.
The Son of God to be made Man,
And man to be made God's own son.

An angel sent by Heavens command
To a spotless virgin in the land;
To one of the seed of David, King,
These joyful tidings for to bring.

He hailed this Virgin, full of grace,
And told Her that in nine month's space,
She should bring forth a Son and He
The Saviour of mankind should be.

When Mary, that most blessed maid,
Heard all the Angel to her said,
She to retirement straight did hie,

The Lord to praise and magnify.

She piously with great content
Each day in contemplation spent;
Until at length the time drew near,
To Bethlehem she did repair.

She, friendless, rangèd up and down
To find a lodging in the town,
But oh! alas! that heavenly guest
No pity found in grief oppressed.

She in pain was forced to hie
Unto a stable that was nigh,
Where of a Son she delivered was
Between an ox and a silly[1] ass.

The spotless mother, wife and maid,
No mortal had to lend her aid;
Exposed to want and piercing cold,
The Lord of life you may behold.

The night of His Nativity
The people in the Heavens did see
Strange wonders which did them surprise,
But none the reason could premise.

The learned men thought it to be
A sign of Cæsars' prosperitie,
But some that notion did control
And said that Isaac had foretold

The coming of this heavenly Boy,
Who would their oracles destroy,
Their magic spells and temples tear,
Which afterwards performèd were.

As earth with a new Son is blessed,
So heaven with a new star is dressed,
The shepherds, warned by an angel, were
To Bethlehem straight to repair.

The shepherds gladly did obey;
To Bethlehem they take their way,
And as the angel did report,
They found the Saviour in that sort

Within a manger there he lay,
His dress was neither rich nor gay,
In Him you truly there might see
A pattern of humility.

Three eastern kings came forth to see
This heavenly Babe come from on high,
Directed by a glorious star
Which they espied from afar.

Their gifts of gold and precious things
They laid before the King of Kings,
Their homage paid with humble heart,
Then joyfully did they depart.

The rumour spread both far and near

Of the Birth of Christ, Our Saviour dear.
That which King Herod came to know,
And strove His work to overthrow.

An angel sent down from on high,
Then ordered Joseph for to fly
To Egypt with Mother and Child,
And there remain for a while.

But Herod full of wrath and gall
Commanded that both great and small,
All under two years old should be
Throughout the land slain instantly.

Deep lamentations you might hear
By every tender mother dear,
To hear their infants' sighs and groans,
Their brains dashed out against the stones.

This massacre was carried on,
Thinking to murder God's own Son;
His persecution soon begun,
But His hour was not yet come.

He in the temple did dispute,
And many errors did confute;
He healed the lepers—raised the dead;
At His command the devils fled.

For all those great and mighty things
Performèd by the King of Kings,

To bring us to the light of grace,
They threw dirt in His Blessed Face.

Let each good Christian great and small
Repair unto the ox's stall:
From those three kings example take;
To this sweet Babe your offering make.

Give Him your heart the first of all,
Free from all malice, wrath and gall.
And now He's on His throne on high,
He will crown you eternally,

97. In the Bleak Mid-Winter

In the bleak mid-winter
Frosty wind made moan;
Earth stood hard as iron,
Water like a stone;
Snow had fallen, snow on snow,
Snow on snow,
In the bleak mid-winter
Long ago.

Our God, heaven cannot hold Him
Nor earth sustain,

Heaven and earth shall flee away
When He comes to reign:
In the bleak mid-winter
A stable-place sufficed
The Lord God Almighty —
Jesus Christ.

Enough for Him, whom cherubim
Worship night and day,
A breastful of milk
And a mangerful of hay;
Enough for Him, whom Angels
Fall down before,
The ox and ass and camel
Which adore.

Angels and Archangels
May have gathered there,
Cherubim and seraphim
Thronged the air;
But only His Mother
In her maiden bliss
Worshipped the Beloved
With a kiss.

What can I give Him,
Poor as I am? —
If I were a Shepherd
I would bring a lamb;

If I were a Wise Man
I would do my part, —
Yet what I can I give Him, —
Give my heart.

98. O Come All Ye Faithful

O come, all ye faithful, joyful and triumphant!
O come ye, O come ye, to Bethlehem
Come and behold Him
Born the King of Angels
O come, let us adore Him
O come, let us adore Him
O come, let us adore Him
Christ the Lord!

God of God, Light of Light
Lo, He abhors not the Virgin's womb
Very God
Begotten, not created
O come, let us adore Him
O come, let us adore Him
O come, let us adore Him
Christ the Lord!

Sing, choirs of angels, sing in exultation
Sing, all ye citizens of heaven above!
Glory to God
All glory in the highest
O come, let us adore Him
O come, let us adore Him
O come, let us adore Him
Christ the Lord!

Yea, Lord, we greet Thee, born this happy morning
Jesus, to Thee be glory given
Word of the Father
Now in flesh appearing
O come, let us adore Him
O come, let us adore Him
O come, let us adore Him
Christ the Lord!

99. What Sweeter Music

What sweeter music can we bring
Than a carol, for to sing
The birth of this our heavenly King?
Awake the voice! Awake the string!

Dark and dull night, fly hence away,
And give the honor to this day,
That sees December turned to May.
That sees December turned to May.

Why does the chilling winter's morn
Smile, like a field beset with corn?
Or smell like a meadow newly-shorn,
Thus, on the sudden? Come and see
The cause, why things thus fragrant be:
'Tis He is born, whose quickening birth
Gives life and luster, public mirth,
To heaven, and the under-earth.

We see him come, and know him ours,
Who, with his sunshine and his showers,
Turns all the patient ground to flowers.
Turns all the patient ground to flowers.
The darling of the world is come,
And fit it is, we find a room
To welcome him. To welcome him.
The nobler part Of all the house here,
Is the heart.

Which we will give him; and bequeath
This holly, and this ivy wreath,
To do him honour, who's our King,
And Lord of all this revelling.

What sweeter music can we bring,
Than a carol for to sing
The birth of this our heavenly King?

100. Sussex Carol

On Christmas night all Christians sing
To hear the news the angels bring
On Christmas night all Christians sing
To hear the news the angels bring

Chorus:
News of great joy news of great mirth
News of our merciful King's birth
When from our sin he set us free
All for to gain our liberty?

Then why should men on earth be so sad
Since our Redeemer made us glad
Then why should men on earth be so sad
Since our Redeemer made us glad Chorus

When sin departs before his grace
Then life and health come in its place

When in its place, angels and men with joy may sing
All for to see the new born King Chorus

All out of darkness we have light
Which made the angels sing this night
Glory to God and peace to men
Now and forever more, Amen.

101. Virgin Unspotted (A Virgin Most Pure)

The Virgin unspotted, the prophets foretold,
Should bring forth a Savior, which now we behold.
To be our Redeemer from death, hell and sin,
Which Adam's transgression involved us in.

Chorus
Therefore let us be merry, cast sorrow away,
Our Saviour Christ Jesus was born on that day.

Through Bethlehem city in Judea it was
That Joseph and Mary together did pass,
And were to be taxed wherever they came,
Since Caesar Augustus condemned the same.

But Mary's full time being came as we find,
She brought forth her first-born to save all mankind,
The in being full for this heavenly guest,
No place could be found to lay him to rest.

But Mary, blest Mary, so meek and so mild,
Soon wrapped in swaddling this heavenly child,
Contented she laid him where oxen were fed,
The great god of mercy approved the deed.

To teach us humility all this was done,
And learn we from hence all imprudence to shun:
A manger His cradle who came from above,
The great God of mercy, of peace, and of love.

Then presently after the shepherds did spy
Vast numbers of Angels to stand in the sky;
How happy they converse, how sweet do they sing,
All glory and praise to our heavenly King.

Printed in Dunstable, United Kingdom